International
Financial Market
Investment

International Financial Market Investment

A SWISS BANKER'S GUIDE

Erwin W. Heri *and* Vanessa Rossi

A Wiley Professional Title

JOHN WILEY & SONS
Chichester • New York • Brisbane • Toronto • Singapore

Original German edition published 1991 under the title o[...]
Was Anleger eigentlich wissen sollten ... by
Helbing and Lichtenhahn Verlag AG, Basel

English translation (modified and updated)
published 1994 by John Wiley & Sons Ltd,
        Baffins Lane, Chichester,
        West Sussex PO19 1UD, England

Copyright © 1991, 1994 Helbing and Lichtenhahn Verlag AG, Basle
                   Switzerland, and Schäffer Verlag
                   für Wirtschaft und Steuern GmbH,
                   Stuttgart, Germany (German editions)

Other Wiley Editorial Offices

John Wiley & Sons, Inc., 605 Third Avenue,
New York, NY 10158-0012, USA

Jacaranda Wiley Ltd, G.P.O. Box 859, Brisbane,
Queensland 4001, Australia

John Wiley & Sons (Canada) Ltd, 22 Worcester Road,
Rexdale, Ontario M9W 1L1, Canada

John Wiley & Sons (SEA) Pte Ltd, 37 Jalan Pemimpin #05-04,
Block B, Union Industrial Building, Singapore 2057

Library of Congress Cataloging-in-Publication Data

Heri, Erwin W.
   [Was Anleger eigentlich wissen sollten. English]
   International financial market investment : a Swiss banker's guide
/ Erwin W. Heri and Vanessa Rossi.
     p.   cm.
   Translation, modified and updated, of: Was Anleger eigentlich
wissen sollten / Erwin W. Heri. 2. Aufl. 1991.
   Includes bibliographical references and index.
   ISBN 0-471-94168-9 (cased)
   1. Investments—Handbooks, manuals, etc.   2. Finance—Handbooks,
manuals, etc.   I. Rossi, Vanessa.   II. Title.
   HG4527.H4613   1993
   332.6—dc20   93—24499
                                             CIP

British Library Cataloguing in Publication Data

A catalogue record for this book is available from the British Library

ISBN 0-471-94168-9

Produced from camera-ready copy supplied by Helbing and Lichtenhahn Verlag AG
Printed and bound in Great Britain by Biddles Ltd, Guildford, Surrey

Contents

Foreword

During recent years, investor interest in the whole range of securities available – shares, bonds, warrants, convertibles and other investment instruments traded in financial markets – has significantly increased. This seems especially true in Europe which may have previously lagged behind the US. Not only have these diverse financial instruments and their respective markets become more actively traded, but popular interest has also grown in their analysis, for instance, the treatment of pricing and risk analysis of such investments.

Most of the basic groundwork for this branch of the 'theory of finance' originates in the US. It is not surprising, therefore, that there are far more general scientific publications on the subject of financial markets available in the US than in Europe. Works aiming at familiarising a wider audience with the rudiments of global financial research are still rather scarce. This book attempts to narrow the gap and to bridge the divide between science and the interested lay person. We know there is a risk that such a project may be doomed to end in failure. For the informed, not only is the material not new, but it may seem trivial, and, given the simplifications used, even questionable. For the newcomer, because of its necessarily technical-sounding language, and despite the attempted simplifications, it may remain out of reach.

The text of this book was originally developed in preparation for a series of lectures on financial markets at the University of Basel which were directed purely at the general public and not at specialists. It should therefore appeal to a wide range of readers: from the least sophisticated private investor, for whom it is an effort to read the economics pages of a daily newspaper and the interest on his savings account is sufficient, to the private investor who is frustrated at missing opportunities such as the massive rise in the Japanese equity market in the 1980s, to the corporate finance director who also 'manages' the company pension fund. Last but not least, this book is also aimed at students who are looking for a brief introduction to the basics of the theory of the financial markets.

This book is therefore not intended for those highly skilled institutional investors who are already fully conversant with sophisticated portfolio management procedures and are no doubt at home in all the futures and options markets. A quick glance at the contents page shows that the most complex instruments are not treated here. Our opinion is clear: futures and options markets, term contracts and other instruments derived from these should not be used by investors until the more traditional instruments explained in this book have been fully understood. It is worth mentioning, however, that it is intended to treat such topics, particularly with reference to portfolio management for institutions (portfolio insurance, portfolio dedication, indexing, etc.) in a later publication.

The main points in this book – as indicated for example in the title of the original German version which translates as, 'What every investor should know' – will be treated using fairly basic terminology. Whilst trying not to be too technical, we will attempt to explain the fundamentals of pricing as well as risk analysis for bonds, shares and exchange rates and to illustrate the use of these basics for portfolio management. We make as much use as possible of simple practical examples to clarify issues.

Whilst the chapter on bonds may seem rather long and, in some cases, the arguments become quite technical for the layman, it should be understood that many of the principles introduced are of wider relevance in investment appraisal, indeed, the equity chapter already refers to results in the preceeding bond chapter. Apart from this 'need to know' justification, investors should be encouraged to follow bond markets for their own sake given that such fixed interest securities form the basis of many savings plans such as pensions, 'income' funds and life insurance policies. This is reflected in the far greater size of world bond markets than equity markets. Even in countries with a strong equity culture, such as the UK, recent trends have generated increased interest in bonds versus equities (not without a heated debate amongst professionals we might add!). The reasons for such a swing in sentiment (in spite of what may seem rather low interest rates on offer) will be better understood by investors familiar with bond pricing and risks as well as equities. Such informed investors may also be wary of being swayed in their own judgment by the recent experience of recession and dividend cuts by companies.

We also believe it essential for investors to understand the rudiments of exchange rate determination and risk. Even if an investor were to avoid investing directly in a foreign market, exchange risks could not be avoided because, in an increasingly interdependent global economy, both domestic markets and domestic company results will be influenced by exchange rates and other external events. Looked at a different way, an investor may see exchange rate fluctuations as an opportunity to enhance returns through foreign investments, including cash positions. The system-atic use of global investment opportunities is treated in the chapter on portfolio theory.

This book is not intended as a guide on how to become rich. This is where it differs from certain works of a popular scientific nature, which purport to do just this. Indeed, in some cases, the authors have in fact become rich. However, we do point out how an investor in volatile markets can avoid making severe mistakes and, perhaps, better understand the functioning and purpose of the various forms of savings and investment from long term pension plans to short term share trading.

It has already been indicated that such an undertaking dictates the use of simplifications which for theoretical purists may even go beyond the bounds of the acceptable. Such purists will have to excuse us.

Our thanks go to our colleagues Marcel Briggen, Lukas Gerig, Gabriel Herrera, Rudi Loertscher and Burkhard Poschadel who read the text and helped clarify points which remained unclear. In addition, we would like to thank Hilary Franks and Andrée Arth for their dedicated assistance and patience in helping with the preparation of this book, including translations from the original German version where necessary. Last but not least, Beverley Pennant and Sue Wyer deserve our gratitude for their patience and skill in typesetting our manuscript – finally there should be no further corrections!

Chapter 1

Introduction

Events in financial markets today play a different role in the consciousness of a broad cross-section of the population than they did 20 years ago. On the one hand, this has to do with the institutional changes in the economic as well as the political environment, and on the other hand, it may also be linked to the fact that the media in recent years have not only improved communications in general, but have also put more emphasis on the reporting of financial market trends.[1]

Alongside the growth in popular interest in economic and financial affairs, the coverage has also become more sophisticated. Clearly, it is no longer considered beyond the knowledge and capabilities of the layman to comprehend quite detailed and technical discussions on such subjects. Thus the degree of numeracy required to follow a systematic treatment of financial markets and investment, such we present in this book, cannot be seen as a barrier for investors motivated to seek a more thorough understanding of the issues.

Before we start evaluating the questions of pricing, risk and portfolio analysis of specific investment instruments (ie. questions of investment in the broadest sense), we will discuss some of the structural factors which have contributed in recent years to the widespread following of financial markets.

International Financing
(by instrument, in US$bn)

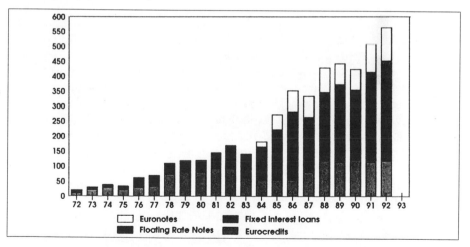

---

[1] Useful reference guides to financial market data include BRETT, M. : 'How to Read the Financial Pages', Century Busines, 3rd Edition 1991, and 'A Guide to Financial Times Statistics' published by the Financial Times Newspaper.

The chart above attempts to illustrate the increased volume of transactions in financial markets, ie. companies raising capital through security issues instead of bank loans on the one hand, and investment in the respective securities by investors on the other.

The chart shows the total amount of international investments made during most of the past 20 years and the partition of financing into some important categories, such as:

- syndicated bank loans
- bonds with fixed interest (straight bonds)
- bonds with variable interest (floating rate notes)
- Euronotes [1]

Two important points can be made from this data:

- The massive increase in financing requirements – especially since 1980, and
- The increasing importance of securities – at the cost of credit financing which from the point of view of investment, is equivalent to substituting bank deposits by investment in securities.

The last point in particular is one aspect of financial market trends which has been intensely discussed in recent years under the title 'Securitisation of debt'.

Amongst other things, 'Securitisation' illustrates the way in which finance, at one time supplied as credit from banks, is now being provided increasingly by securities. Looking at the other side of the coin, it also illustrates the savers' shift away from savings deposits, which at one time provided banks with the potential for supplying credit, towards investment in securities, typically offering much higher expected returns. These structural changes in financing as well as investment habits have made it necessary to rethink and reorganise both the commercial and securities businesses of the banking sector. Furthermore, this form of company financing, together with risk trading, has led to strong growth in the respective securities markets.

This growth is often compared with the growth in the real economy and differences in growth often lead to fears of some kind of potential danger which could result from an 'unbalanced' development in financial markets. The substitution effect described above – credit substituted by securities financing, savings accounts by securities

---

[1] Euronotes are short to medium term bonds (RUFs, NIFs etc.) with or without a 'standby agreement' from banks (so-called Eurocommercial Paper).

Chapter 2

Bonds

1. Introduction

A bond is a debt certificate and its simplest form provides for regular payments to the holder. As a rule, such a debt certificate is written in the name of the holder and, also as a rule, a number of conditions for this certificate are attached on issue of the paper, for example the amount of interest (coupon), date of repayment of principal, alternative repayment possibilities, etc.

It may have been noticed that we have used the term 'as a rule' quite often already. This is to do with the fact that, in recent years, we have seen many innovations in bond markets. Indeed, it may soon be justified to use instead of 'as a rule' the statement 'the case illustrated by so-called straight bonds' as these are slowly becoming the exception in the markets, at least in the most recent issue statistics.

Bonds are by far the most significant vehicle of investment in the world. World bond market capitalisation exceeds world equity market capitalisation by a long way and outside capital in the form of bonds plays a much more important role than share capital in the financing of companies. The appearance of so-called 'junk bonds', and, especially in the USA, the increase in the number of companies buying back their own shares has even accentuated the outstanding importance of bonds in relation to equities. This dominance is also reflected in the securities portfolios of institutional and private investors alike. A further pressure towards such asset allocation across portfolios is seen in the form of regulatory frameworks, for example, in the invest-ment regulations of pension funds in Switzerland a maximum of 30% of a portfolio may be held in equities, but up to 100% in fixed interest instruments. Similar regulations are also valid in Germany and a number of other countries although adjustments to these regulations have tended to ease restrictions in favour of equities, and derivatives, in recent years.

These portfolio preferences and regulatory regimes are linked to the common belief that bonds are a less risky investment than shares. Indeed, from the basic description, it may appear as if bonds are very similar to special savings deposit accounts, with 'penalties' imposed for early withdrawal. Regular interest payments provide an income stream suited to pension plans and the longer life of a bond should provide a better guarantee of this income than potentially volatile short-term deposit rates. However, the assumption that, as with a savings account, the principal invested can always be recovered in full is not necessarily true and bonds are not as riskfree as the simple description may suggest.

We will learn in the following chapters that risk considerations will have to be thought of in relative terms, and we will also see that the well-known proverb, 'he who eats well buys shares, and he who sleeps well buys bonds', does not necessarily hold in all circumstances. There are circumstances for both investments in which one may not only sleep badly, but also suffer loss of appetite. This is linked not only to the fact that we have had to learn to live with an important increase in general interest rate volatility in the last ten years, together with an increasing price risk in fixed interest investment, but also, given the growth in certain M&A (Mergers & Acquisitions) activities (eg. leveraged buy-outs), to the fact that the borrower risk may increase to such an extent that the interest rate on a specific bond may no longer be constant during the entire lifespan of the bond, even if general rates are steady. Before delving into such complex issues, we will take a brief look at the types of bonds typically found in the markets.

Putting to one side the numerous complex innovations developed in recent years in the capital markets, then we can identify three broad categories of bonds:

- Domestic bonds
- Foreign bonds
- Eurobonds

The following table describes the most important distinctions between these different bonds:

Most important characteristics	Domestic bonds	Foreign bonds	Eurobonds
Domicile of borrower	Onshore	Offshore	Offshore
Consortium for issue	Domestic	Abroad	International
Tax deduction on interest (withholding tax)	Yes, as a rule eg Japan 20% US 30% UK 25% Germany 25% Switzerland 35%	No	No
Secondary market/most frequent way of trading internationally	Quotes and dealing on domestic market	Quotes and dealing in country of issue	International telephone dealing (regulated by ISMA*)

ISMA = International Securities Market Association

Depending on the regulatory environment in a particular country, one category may play a more important role than others. For instance, Euro-SFr-bonds, due to restrictions by the Swiss National Bank (and agreements with foreign central banks), are prohibited, therefore SFr-foreign bonds play an unusually important role; in another example an instrument may be permitted only as an issue for supranational borrowers (some restrictions of this kind have been seen in Austria).

On the following pages are some examples of bond sales advertisements – they are sales offers in the broadest sense. The advertisements act as examples for us to look at some of the properties of bonds. The first advertisement (the English version is given as well as the German language version from original offer documents) gives information about the borrower – the City of Yokohama – and particulars of the bonds on offer. It is a so-called 'straight bond' of a first-class (AAA) borrower, with a 5% coupon and a maturity of 10 years. In the first box there is a clear description of the bonds with maturity, issue price, coupon, repayments, etc. which is followed by another summary of the purchase offer, as well as a list of the banks which have committed themselves to underwrite (guarantee sale of) the bonds and offer them to their clients.

This is a typical bond advertisement, found almost daily in newspapers. From the example of the City of Yokohama bonds, we will try, in the following sections, to evaluate a number of principles of bond analysis, particularly pricing and risk evaluation.

The City of Yokohama
Japan
Guaranteed by
The Japanese government

5% Bonds 1987-97 of SFr 100,000,000

Issue price:	100.25% + 0.3% tax on negotiation of securities
Life:	Maximum 10 years
Settlement date:	10 December 1987
Redemption:	The City of Yokohama has the right to repay the bonds according to sections 3 and 5 of the Terms of the Bonds. Final redemption on 10 December 1997.
Delivery of bonds:	As soon as possible
Sales restrictions:	USA & Japan

The banks named below have purchased these Bonds and offer them for public subscription until 27 November 1987, noon.

Credit Suisse	**Union Bank of Switzerland**	**Swiss Bank Corporation**
Bank of Tokyo (Schweiz) AG		**Yokohama Finanz (Schweiz) AG**
Swiss Volksbank	**Bank Leu Ltd.**	**Members of the Groupement des Banquiers Privés Genevois**
Bank Sarasin & Cie	**Private Bank and Trust Company**	**Members of the Groupement de Banquiers Privés Zurichois**
Swiss Cantonalbanks		**Banca della Svizzera Italiana**
Bank Hoffman Ltd	**Bank Cantrade Ltd.**	**Swiss Deposit and Creditbank**
Banque Romande		

The Nikko (Switzerland) Finance Co., Ltd.	**Nomura (Switzerland) Ltd.**

Swiss Security   No. 769 592

The City of Yokohama
Japan

mit Solidarbürgschaft der japanischen Regierung

5% Anleihe 1987-97 von SFr 100,000,000

- Die City of Yokohama ist eine lokale, öffentliche Körperschaft mit einer von der japanischen Verfassung garantierten Autonomie.
- Mit rund 3,1 Millionen Einwohnern ist Yokohama die zweitgrösste Stadt Japans.
- Yokohama besitzt den grössten Hafen Japans.

Laufzeit:	längstens 10 Jahre
Emissionspreis:	100.25% + 0.3% eidg. Umsatzabgabe
Coupons:	5% p.a., zahlbar jährlich am 10 Dezember
Rückzahlung:	spätestens 10 Dezember 1997

Vorzeitige Rückzahlungsmöglichkeiten:

(a) Unter Einhaltung einer Kündigungsfrist von mindestens 60 Tagen ohne Grundangabe ab 10. Dezember 1992 zu 101.50% (degressiv $1/_2$% p.a.) und ab 10. Dezember 1994 zu 100,50% (degressiv $1/_4$% p.a. bis zum Nennwert).

(b) Bei Einführung einer Quellensteuer in Japan ist die Emittentin berechtigt, unter Einhaltung einer Kündigungsfrist von mindestens 60 Tagen sämtliche Obligationen zurückzuzahlen. Eine solche Rückzahlung kann ab 10. Dezember 1988 zu 102% erfolgen, mit jährlich $1/_2$% degressiven Prämien bis zum Nennwert, zuzüglich der bis zum Rückzahlungstermin aufgelaufenen Zinsen.

Sicherstellung:

(a) Solidarbürgschaft der japanischen Regierung
(b) Negativklausel

Stückelung:	Titel zu SFr 5,000 und SFr 100,000
Zeichnungsschluss:	27. November 1987, mittags
Liberierung:	10. Dezember 1987

Steuerstatus: Jegliche Zahlung von Zinsen, Kapital und allfällgen Prämien erfolgt ohne Abzug von irgendwelchen an der Quelle zurückbehaltenen gegenwärtigen oder zukünftigen Steuern, Abgaben oder Gebühren.

Verkaufsrestriktionen: Japan und Vereinigte Staaten von Amerika

Zeichnungsangebot

Die unterzeichneten Institute haben die vorbeschriebene

5% Anleihe 1987-97 von SFr 100,000,000
der City of Yokohama, Japan
mit Solidarbürgschaft der japanischen Regierung

fest übernommen und legen sie bis zum

27 November 1987, mittags

zu den nachstehenden Bedingungen zur öffentlichen Zeichnung auf:

1. Der **Emissionspreis** beträgt **100.25%**, zuzüglich 0.3% eidg. Umsatzabgabe.

2. Die **Zeichnungen** werden durch die schweizerischen Geschäftsstellen der unterzeichneten Institute spesenfrei entgegengenommen.

3. Die **Zuteilung** steht im Ermessen der untenstehenden Institute. Sie werden die Zeichner so bald als möglich nach Zeichnungsschluss hierüber unterrichten.

4. Die **Liberierung** der zugeteilten Titel hat am 10 Dezember 1987 zu erfolgen.

5. Die **Titel** werden so bald als möglich geliefert.

6. **Verkaufsrestriktionen:** Japan und Vereinigte Staaten von Amerika.

19 November 1987

Schweizerische Kreditanstalt	**Schweizerische Bankgesellschaft**	**Schweizerischer Bankverein**
Bank of Tokyo (Schweiz) AG		**Yokohama Finanz (Schweiz) AG**
Schweizerische Volksbank	**Bank Leu AG**	**Vereinigung der Genfer Privatbankiers**
Bank Sarasin & Cie	**Privatbank & Verwaltungsgesellschaft**	**Gruppe Zürcher Privatbankiers**
Schweizerische Kantonalbanken		**Banca della Svizzera Italiana**
Bank Hoffmann AG	**Bank Cantrade AG**	**Schweizerische Depositen- und Kreditbank**
Banque Romande		

The Nikko (Switzerland) Finance Co, Ltd.   **Nomura (Switzerland) Ltd.**

Valoren Nr.: 769.592   Zeichnungsscheine für diese Anleihe können bei den obenerwähnten Instituten bezogen werden.

PRUDENTIAL FUNDING CORPORATION
(incorporated in the State of New Jersey, U.S.A)

A subsidiary of

The **Prudential**  Insurance Company of America

US$ 200,000,000
8¹/₄% per cent Notes due 1995

Issue Price 101.305 per cent

Interest on the Notes is payable annually in arrears on 9 August, commencing 9 August 1992. The Notes will mature on 9 August 1995 and will be repaid at par.

The Notes are not subject to redemption prior to maturity except that they may be redeemed in whole at par plus accrued interest at any time if certain events occur involving United States taxation or information reporting requirements as set forth herein.

Application has been made to the Council of the International Stock Exchange of the United Kingdom and the Republic of Ireland Limited ('the London Stock Exchange') in London for the Notes to be admitted to the Official List. Copies of this document, which comprises listing particulars with regard to the issue of the Notes, have been prepared in accordance with the listing rules made under Section 142 of the Financial Services Act 1986 and have been delivered to the Registrar of Companies for registration in accordance with Section 149 of that Act.

The Notes have not been, and will not be, registered under the United States Securities Act of 1933, and are subject to US tax law requirements. Subject to certain exceptions, Notes may not be offered, sold or delivered within the United States or to US persons.

The Notes will initially be represented by a single temporary Global Note, in bearer form without interest coupons, to be deposited with a common depositary outside the United States for Morgan Guaranty Trust Company of New York, Brussels office, as operator of the Euroclear System and CEDEL S.A. on or about 9 August 1991. Except as otherwise provided herein, the temporary Global Note will be exchangeable for definitive Notes on or after 40 days after delivery of and payment for the temporary Global Note upon certification as to non-US beneficial ownership.

Swiss Bank Corporation

Bankers Trust International Limited	Banque Bruxelles Lambert S.A.
Credit Suisse First Boston Limited	Deutsche Bank Capital Markets Limited
Kidder, Peabody International Limited	Kuwait International Investment Co. (S.A.K.)
Lehman Brothers International	J.P. Morgan Securities Ltd.
Merrill Lynch International Limited	Nomura International
Prudential-Bache Securities	Salomon Brothers International Limited

UBS Phillips & Drew Securities Limited

Offering Circular dated 2 August 1991

OFFERING CIRCULAR SUMMARY

Prudential Funding Corporation

Prudential Funding Corporation (the 'Company' or 'Prudential Funding') is a corporation incorporated in the State of New Jersey. The Company is a wholly-owned subsidiary of PRUCO, Inc., which in turn is a wholly-owned subsidiary of The Prudential Insurance Company of America ('The Prudential'). The Company serves as a financing company for The Prudential and its subsidiaries.

The Issue

Issuer:	Prudential Funding Corporation
Securities:	US$ 200,000,000 81/4% per cent. Notes due 1995
Amount:	US$ 200,000,000
Issue price:	101.305 per cent
Interest:	The Notes will bear interest from 9 August 1991, at the rate of 81/4 per cent per annum, payable annually in arrears on each 9 August commencing on 9 August 1992.
Maturity:	9 August 1995
Optional redemption:	None, except for redemption for tax or information reporting reasons
Tax/information reporting redemption:	The Notes may be redeemed in whole at par plus accrued interest at any time if certain events occur involving United States taxation or information reporting requirements
Form:	The Notes will be represented initially by a single temporary Global Note in bearer form without interest coupons (the 'Global Note'), which will be deposited on or about 9 August 1991 with a common depositary outside the United States for Morgan Guaranty Trust Company of New York, Brussels office, as operator of the Euroclear System, and for CEDEL S.A. for the accounts of the subscribers of the Notes. Except as otherwise provided herein the Global Note may be surrendered outside the United States to the Fiscal and Paying Agent to be exchanged, in whole or in part, for definitive Notes on or after 40 days after delivery of and payment for the temporary Global Note upon certification as to non-US beneficial ownership or otherwise as required by US Treasury regulations and Regulation S under the US Securities Act of 1933, as provided in the Fiscal Agency Agreement. A beneficial owner must cause his share of the Global Note to be exchanged for definitive Notes before interest can be collected
Listing:	The London Stock Exchange
Rating:	The Notes have been rated AAA by Standard & Poor's Corporation and Aa1 by Moody's Investors Service
Support agreement:	The Notes will be guaranteed by The Prudential but the Company has a support agreement with The Prudential, as more particularly described on page 12 hereof
Governing law:	New York

British Gas International Finance B.V.
(incorporated in The Netherlands with limited liability and having its statutory seat in The Hague)

C$ 250,000,000
$10^1/_8$ per cent Guaranteed Bonds due 1998

Guaranteed by

British Gas public limited company
(incorporated in England and Wales with limited liability on 1 April 1986)
(registered number 2006000)

Issue Price 101.55 per cent

Application has been made to the Council of The International Stock Exchange of the United Kingdom and the Republic of Ireland Limited ('The Stock Exchange') for the Bonds to be admitted to the Official List. Copies of this document have been delivered to the Registrar of Companies in England and Wales as required by Section 149 of the Financial Services Act 1986.

Interest on the Bonds will be payable annually in arrears on 13 March, the first payment to be made on 13 March 1992. Payments on the Bonds will be made without deduction for or on account of taxes of The Netherlands or the United Kingdom as described under 'Terms and Conditions of the Bonds - Taxation'.

The Bonds mature on 13 March 1998, but may be redeemed before then, in whole but not in part, at the option of the Issuer at any time at their principal amount together with accrued interest in the event of certain changes affecting taxes of The Netherlands or the United Kingdom as described under 'Terms and Conditions of the Bonds – Redemption and Purchase'.

The Bonds will initially be represented by a Temporary Global Bond, without Coupons, which will be deposited with a common depositary on behalf of CEDEL S.A. and Morgan Guaranty Trust Company of New York, Brussels office, as operator of the Euroclear System ('Euroclear') on or about 13 March 1991 (the 'Closing Date'). The Temporary Global Bond will be exchangeable for definitive Bonds in bearer form in the denominations of C$ 1,000 and C$ 10,000 each with Coupons attached following the expiration of 40 days after the Closing Date, upon presentation of certificates in a form required by United States tax laws as to non-US beneficial ownership.

Swiss Bank Corporation

ABN AMRO	**Bankers Trust International Limited**
Credit Suisse First Boston Limited	**Goldman Sachs International Limited**

Scotia McLeod Inc.

BMO Nesbitt Thomson Ltd	**Banque Bruxelles Lambert S.A.**
Banque Internationale à Luxembourg S.A.	**Crédit Lyonnais**
Daiwa Europe Limited	**Dresdner Bank Aktiengesellschaft**
Fuji International Finance Limited	**Generale Bank**
Hambros Bank Limited	**Kredietbank International Group**
Nomura International	**Rabobank Nederland**

Wood Grundy Inc

Offering Circular dated 8 March 1991

2. Pricing

The issue price of our City of Yokohama (CoY) bonds is 100.25%. This means, for a bond of SFr 5,000, an investor has to pay SFr 5,012.50, plus a Swiss turnover tax of SFr 15 (the Swiss stamp duty). In the quoted offer, the City of Yokohama (together with the Japanese State, which takes on a joint guarantee) takes on the duty of repaying the SFr 5,000 on 10.12.1997. For the duration of the bond, SFr 250 interest payment is due each year, always on 10 December.

This investment seems to be relatively risk-free. One invests SFr 5,012.50 receives SFr 250 in interest every year and gets the SFr 5,000 back in exactly ten years. Such risk considerations are responsible for the fact that bonds from quality debtors are generally viewed as risk-free. This view is true in a certain sense. However, under two conditions, this can be a fallacy for the investor. Firstly, if the debtor, despite his present credit rating, gets into difficulties with payments during the following years – we will return to this problem later – and secondly, if the creditor, ie. the investor, for whatever reasons suddenly needs his money back within the duration of the credit. In this case, he normally goes to the secondary market and might, under the circumstances, find out that within the duration of the credit, even with no problems over the borrower's standing, he will not necessarily get his full SFr 5,000 back. Under these circumstances, he will find out just how much the price of a bond can fluctuate within the (ten-year) maturity.

The chart below shows the actual fluctuations of the CoY bond price from January 1988 until December 1991.

5% City of Yokohama bond price (left)   Average yield on Swiss bonds (right)

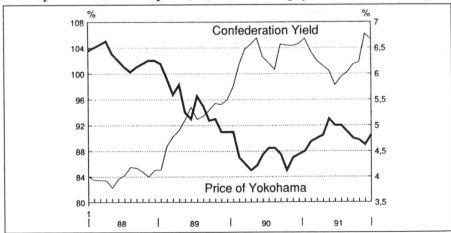

The graph clearly shows that the bonds opened on the secondary market at a price of over 100, but then systematically lost value and were only around 85 (ie. a loss of 15%) around April and October 1990. It can also be seen from the graph that the loss in value corresponded with a systematic increase in the average yield of Swiss franc bonds in the Swiss market, ie. general interest rates. We will see later that this negative correlation between a bond price and the general interest rate level is systematic in every economy. Furthermore, it is obvious here that even if the (contractual) interest payments are made regularly and the SFr 5,000 will be paid back after ten years, the intervening market price fluctuations of the bonds can still be enormous. An investor who bought the CoY bonds in December 1987 and sold them in April 1990 would have received only SFr 4,250 in the market instead of the SFr 5,000 that was initially invested, although the borrower's quality was still AAA, ie. unchanged.

These considerations make it obvious that an investor has to take into account the determinants of the actual market value of bonds during their lifetime in order not to be unpleasantly surprised.

In general, the market value of bonds crucially depends on two separate categories of influential factors:

- Bond-specific factors such as the interest coupon, (time to) maturity, the repayment sum, borrower's standing, etc.

- The actual market interest rate which is largely determined by the fundamental economic environment.

A number of these influential factors are themselves variable over time and influence the value of bonds in such a way that price fluctuations cannot be avoided. Later on, we will evaluate methods for determining the price of bonds. However, for this, we need to use certain basic principles for calculating present values and compound interest. As these principles may not be immediately familiar to all readers, we will allow ourselves a brief explanatory digression.[1]

Digression: calculating compound interest and present values

The concept of 'present value' is a way of assessing the value of a stream of future payments through the calculation of an 'equivalent' present lump sum, with the interest rate used to 'discount' the future income as this clearly represents the trade-

---

[1] If the mathematical expressions over the next three pages appear tedious, we would encourage readers to at least glance at the examples given.

off between money today and money tomorrow. However, to arrive at the expression for the 'present value', we will start by defining 'future value'. The 'future value' of a present sum X in one year's time is the amount of money generated if X is invested for one year at an interest rate r. As a rule, the 'future value' is called FV (Future Value) and the value of the present amount X is called PV ('Present Value').

This means:

$$
\begin{aligned}
FV &= PV + \text{Interest on PV} \\
&= PV + r \cdot PV \\
&= PV\,(1+r)
\end{aligned}
$$

If we consider a maturity of two years rather than one, and keep the interest rate constant, it then follows that:

$$
FV = PV + r \cdot PV \qquad\qquad + \qquad\qquad r \cdot (PV + r \cdot PV)
$$

$$
\underbrace{\qquad\qquad}_{\substack{\text{Interest in} \\ \text{1st year}}} \qquad\qquad\qquad \underbrace{\qquad\qquad}_{\substack{\text{Interest in} \\ \text{2nd year}}}
$$

$$
\begin{aligned}
&= PV + r \cdot PV + r \cdot PV + r^2 \cdot PV \\
&= PV\,(1+2r+r^2) \\
&= (1+r)^2\,PV \quad {}^{[1]}
\end{aligned}
$$

If we extend this to an arbitrary number of periods (n), and again keep the interest rate constant over the whole period, the future value of an initial amount of PV invested at an interest rate r becomes

(E1) $$FV = (1+r)^n\,PV$$

If we now think of a given amount FV available in the future in terms of its present value, then this present amount can be expressed as follows:

(E2) $$PV = \frac{1}{(1+r)^n}\,FV$$

This equation (E2) is simply the previous equation for FV (E1) inverted to solve for PV.

---

[1]   In full, $(1+r)^2 = (1+r)(1+r) = 1+r+r+r^2 = (1+2r+r^2)$.

A simple example: Suppose that because of known plans, such as retirement, we want to receive the sum of US$ 100,000 (FV) in five years' time (n=5) and assume an interest rate of 12%, then, taking into account all interest and compound interest, we would today have to invest at 12% the amount of US$ 56,743:

$$ PV = \frac{1}{(1+0.12)^5} \times 100,000 = 56,743 $$

Clearly the interest rate (r) plays an important part. The higher it is, the higher the future value becomes for any given starting value. Alternatively, the corresponding starting value becomes smaller for a given future value.

In connection with bond pricing, the present and future values are of great importance. For 'normal' bonds, ie. the 'straight bonds', it is particularly these present and future values of so-called annuities which matter. If we were to analyse somewhat more special forms of loans, then so-called perpetuities become significant.

An **Annuity** is a number of payments (for instance interest payments) of a fixed amount F over a certain period (eg. n years). In contrast, a **Perpetuity** is an infinite number of payments of a fixed amount F per period.[1]

A simple example, in brief, of the present and future values of an annuity:

For three years at the end of each year, SFr1,000 is paid on a bond held and this sum is transferred into an account paying 4% interest per annum. How much has been saved after 3 years? The following table gives an overview of the flows arising and sums generated:

Year	0	1	2	3
Payment		1,000	1,000	1,000
Value of year 2 payment in year 3 $\longrightarrow$			$\rightarrow$ x 1.04 $\longrightarrow$	1,040
Value of year 1 payment in year 3 $\longrightarrow$		$\rightarrow$ x 1.04	$\longrightarrow$ x 1.04 $\longrightarrow$	1,081.60
Total saved after 3 years				**3,121.60**

---

[1] It should not be difficult to see the similarity between these instruments and a pension plan (which guarantees a certain income payment for n years, where n is uncertain depending on death of recipient).

In general, the future value of an annuity (FVA) of A per period over n periods at an interest rate of r is

(E3)
$$\text{FVA} = A \sum_{t=1}^{n} (1+r)^{n-t} = \left\{ \frac{(1+r)^n - 1}{r} \right\} A$$

Taking the above example with n=3, r=4%, gives:

$$\text{FVA} = 1000 \sum_{t=1}^{3} 1.04^{3-t} = 1000 \left\{ \frac{1.04^3 - 1}{0.04} \right\} = 3121.60$$

What does the present value of the above example look like? ie. what is the present value of a payment of SFr 1,000 each year over three years?

Year	0	1	2	3
Payment		1,000	1,000	1,000

$$961.50 \longleftarrow \; x\left(\frac{1}{1.04}\right) \longleftarrow$$

$$924.55 \longleftarrow \qquad\qquad x\left(\frac{1}{1.04^2}\right) \longleftarrow$$

$$889.00 \longleftarrow \qquad\qquad\qquad\qquad\qquad x\left(\frac{1}{1.04^2}\right) \longleftarrow$$

Present value   **2775.00**

In general, the present value of an annuity (PVA) of A per period after n periods at an interest rate of r equals

(E4) $$\text{PVA} = A \sum_{t=1}^{n} \frac{1}{(1+r)^t} = \left\{ \frac{1}{r} - \frac{1}{r(1+r)^n} \right\} A$$

Using the above example with n=3, r=4%, this corresponds to:

$$\text{PVA} = 1000 \sum_{t=1}^{3} \frac{1}{1.04^t} = 1000 \left\{ \frac{1}{1.04} - \frac{1}{1.04\,(1.04)^3} \right\} = 2775$$

In this case, an investor would have to pay an initial sum of SFr 2775 to secure a payment of SFr 1000 per annum for three years. If the investor could actually obtain an interest rate of 5% on his money, the annuity would be a poor investment. On the contrary, if the alternative rate was 4% in the first year but 3% thereafter, the annuity would be good value.   **- End of digression -**

Returning now to the CoY bonds discussed earlier, and again looking at the credit conditions, these contain an annuity – the promise of payment of a fixed amount of interest annually – of SFr 250 per year, together with the promise to pay the amount of SFr 5,000 at the end of 10 years (n=10). These ('straight') bonds therefore comprise an annuity amounting to the coupon payment (C) and a sum amounting to the repayment (T), fixed in advance.

Expressed in terms used in the above digression, the value of the annuity (compare to (E4)) is

(i)
$$PVA = C \sum_{t=1}^{n} \frac{1}{(1+r)^t}$$

where C is the coupon amount and n the (remainder of) time to maturity of the bonds. The present value of the repayment (T) (compare to (E2)) is

(ii)
$$PVR = T \frac{1}{(1+r)^n}$$

Consequently, the value of a bond ie. its present value, PV, represents the sum of these two present values, PVA plus PVR:

(2.1)
$$PV = C \sum_{t=1}^{n} \frac{1}{(1+r)^t} + T \frac{1}{(1+r)^n}$$

This equation can be simplified[1] as:

(2.2)
$$PV = \frac{C}{r} + \frac{1}{(1+r)^n} \left\{ T - \frac{C}{r} \right\}$$

---

[1] The transformation of (2.2) may not immediately appear to be a simplification to everyone. However, there are no more summation signs left in (2.2), which is a significant simplification for the calculation of the price of bonds with a long time to run to maturity (n).

Where

PV	=	Calculated price of a bond
C	=	Coupon payment
r	=	Market interest rate
n	=	(Time to) maturity
T	=	Repayment amount

Except for the market interest rate, all parameters for our CoY bonds are set in the prospectus. If we now use the market interest rate valid at the time of issue of 4.97% – we will come back to the meaning of this market interest rate – we can calculate the issue price given in the prospectus:

$$\text{Issue price CoY} = \frac{5000}{0.0497} + \frac{1}{(1.0497)^{10}} \left\{ 100\,000 - \frac{5000}{0.0497} \right\}$$

$$= \quad 100{,}240 \text{ for } 100{,}000$$
$$(\text{price set } 100.25\%)$$

In the same way, the 'correct' theoretical price for any simple promise of payment, for any type of bond, can be determined. It corresponds to the value of all future payments (ie. promises of payment) discounted to the present period. We will talk about the discount rate and the interest rate to be used in more detail at a later stage. To determine the price of new bonds in the market, an analyst or investor would initially make use of the yield on existing bonds issued by the same borrower, although this may not always be possible (eg. if such do not exist or if they have different conditions attached). The important point here is that today's price of any bond corresponds to the present value of all future payments.

3. Yield to maturity

In the above example, we assumed that we knew the current market interest rate on issue and based on this we could calculate the value, ie. price, of the bond. In reality, the market interest rate may not be available. Only the market value (price P) of the bonds may be given, either because this is fixed by the issuing institution (taking into consideration the relevant market conditions), or because the bonds are already traded in the secondary market (or perhaps even in the grey market), and the prices are published in the newspaper. In this case, either equation (2.1) or (2.2) would have to be solved to determine the interest rate. The result would be that interest rate for which the present value of the future flow of payments (coupon payments plus repayment) would equal the (published) price of the bonds. For reasons which will be explained later, this interest rate is called **yield to maturity**. Exact solutions of equations such as (2.2) for the yield to maturity r can only be found using an iterative method. However, there are a number of approximate solutions with sufficient accuracy to make the usual investment decisions. One of the most simple forms of equation used to calculate the 'yield to maturity' or 'internal rate of return', as it is sometimes called, is:

$$(2.3) \qquad\qquad r \approx \frac{C + (T\text{-}P) / n}{P}$$

Again, we take our CoY bonds and assume as an example that we are going to buy them in April 1989 at a market value of 96. Approximately what yield to maturity can an investor expect if he keeps them from April 1989 to maturity, ie. December 1997 (time to maturity = 8.6 years)?

$$r = 5000 + \frac{(100\,000 - 96\,000) / 8.6}{96\,000} = 0.057$$

Obviously, this yield, 5.7%, is higher than the coupon of 5% initially offered. This is because the bonds are 'below par' (ie. price less than 100) one year after issue. This means that after one year, an investor has the right to future interest payments as stated in the contract, as well as the repayment of SFr 5,000 in 1997, but buying this 'right' is cheaper than before. We will look at some of the reasons for this.

Let us summarise the concept of the yield to maturity:

The yield to maturity is that interest rate which equates the present value (PV) of all future payments of a bond (interest payments and repayments) with the market value (P) of the bond. Possible changes in value up to maturity due to coupon variations are also included in the calculation.

From this we can draw three concrete conclusions:

- If the bonds are at par value (100%), then the yield to maturity is equal to the coupon interest (nominal interest). Possible increases in value or losses in value before the maturity date are not considered.

- If a bond is below par, as in the above example, then the yield to maturity is above the nominal interest rate, as there will be a gain in value in addition to the coupon and payment on maturity.

- If a bond is above par, then the yield to maturity is below the nominal interest rate of the bond, because there will be a loss in value before maturity.

Considering the compound interest philosophy, it is doubtless reasonable to use the concept of yield to maturity to assess the price of bonds. But it also turns out that relatively strong assumptions have to be made when using this pricing concept. For example, the simplified formula above is not only based on the assumption that during the whole life of the bond, all coupon payments are reinvested, but it is also implicitly assumed that during the life of the bond, all coupon payments are invested **at the same interest rate** as the yield to maturity. Clearly, interest rate volatility in recent years has made us all well aware that this last assumption is not really justified. This is quite apart from the fact that coupon payments are often just 'left' in bank accounts, or are even used as income for consumer spending. Under such circumstances, of course, the ex-post yield of a bond can be quite different from the previously calculated yield-to-maturity. These questions have led to the recent development of alternative yield concepts. These concepts, as a rule, make use of the knowledge that the so-called 'Yield Curve' contains information about interest rates in the future.

From the yield curve, which depicts nothing but a snap-shot cross-section of actual market yields of bonds across various (times to) maturities, an investor can calculate something approximating market expectations of future interest rates. As these estimated future interest rates are quite likely to differ from actual prevailing interest rates, it is already clear that the yield result will be different from the result obtained using the simplified formula for the yield to maturity (and more realistic, as a rule). It would be going too far to delve into more detail here about these more complex calculations. But it is important at least to realise that the yield to maturity is, in principle, an **expected yield**. The actual yield achieved ex post can differ significantly from the expected yield to maturity, depending on the coupon payments and the interest rates at which payments are reinvested over the life of the bond.

4. Determining factors for bond prices

It has already been pointed out that the market value of a bond depends firstly on the security-specific factors such as interest coupon, (time to) maturity, repayment sum, borrower's standing, etc., and secondly on market interest rates, and the general economic environment. In the following sections, we will consider briefly the influences of these individual factors. Technically speaking, we will examine what the sign is of the first derivative of the price in equations (2.1) and (2.2) with respect to the different arguments in the equations.

4.1 Market value: dependency on coupon and final repayment

Basically, the coupon (nominal interest), together with the repayment sum, both have a positive influence on market value. If we assume that all bonds have the same debtor risk (we will come back to this assumption), then all bonds of equal maturity should have identical yields. Thus, under these particular conditions, bonds with a 10% coupon will be more expensive (higher current value) than those with an 8% coupon. In other words, in efficient markets, prices will be fixed in such a way that both bonds will have approximately the same yield. All other things being equal, then at a market interest rate of 8%, bonds with an 8% coupon would be traded at par, those with a higher coupon above par, and those with a lower coupon than 8% would be traded below par.

The same would hold true for the repayment amount. In theory the repayment amount (the lump sum which is paid back to the investor at final maturity) can be larger or smaller than the lump sum paid in at the issuing date. A bond with a final repayment above face value would be priced above par and one with a final repayment below face value would be priced below par, ceteris paribus.

4.2 Market value: dependency on remainder of the term

The coupon and repayment sum are both, as a rule, fixed by contract (exception: floating rate notes), and they remain constant until maturity. As long as no other factors influence the market value, the price level of a bond, under the influence of the steadily decreasing remainder of term, tends towards the repayment price. If the market value of a bond is, at some intermediate stage, above the repayment amount, then the value should decrease gradually over time, until it converges with the repayment amount at maturity. Conversely, the market value increases steadily until maturity if it is at some prior date less than the repayment amount.

4.3 Market value: dependency on borrower's credit rating

A borrower's rating (credit-worthiness) is understood to be the credit capability of a borrower, ie. the probability of the borrower being able to fulfil all the future obligations connected with the bonds (coupon payments and repayment). The lower the estimation of the borrower's standing, the higher the 'risk premium' would become for the investor to take on the corresponding credit. Most bonds are given credit-ratings by either specialised rating-agencies or major banks throughout the world. These ratings, normally based on the fundamental strength of the issuer of a bond, are an indicator of the probability of a borrower meeting his future obligations. The lower the rating, the higher the interest rate to be paid by the borrower. That is to say, the lower the present value of a promise of payment in the future (taking uncertainty into account), the lower the market value of the bonds. The ratings definitions of the two most prestigious ratings companies (Moody's and Standard & Poor's) are summarised in the table opposite.[1]

---

[1]   For a detailed analysis and description see: Bond Ratings and Bond Rating Outlines in 'The Financial Analyst's Handbook' edited by LEVINE, S.E., Second Edition Business One Irwin, 1988.

Bond-Rating

Definition
Degree of probability of full payment
of capital and interest of a bond
(Bonds from the same debtors can have different ratings
due to different guarantees)

Standard & Poor's		Moody's	
AAA	**Extraordinarily large capacity** for servicing of interest and capital payments	AAA	**Top** quality
AA	**Very large** capacity for interest and debt servicing	AA	**Good** quality in **all** aspects
A	**Large** capacity for interest and debt servicing, but **less favourable economic conditions** than AAA and AA	A	Many **favourable** investment characteristics, **upper market category**
BBB	**Acceptable capacity** for interest and debt servicing	BAA	**Middle quality**
BB, B, CCC, CC	Mostly **speculative** with varying degrees of uncertainty regarding interest and debt servicing	BA	**Speculative** element
C	'Income bonds' [1], for which **no interest** is paid	B	In general, such bonds do not have the properties of a recommended bond: **not recommended**
D	**In default**	CAA	**Poor** rating
		CA	**Highly speculative** character
		C	**Lowest** valued category

---

[1] For 'income bonds', interest is only paid if profits are actually earned by the debtor.

Based on these rating categories, the following chart gives an indication of the scale of risk premiums that had to be paid in the past by the various risk categories. This clearly shows that the worse the debtor's rating, the higher the interest he has had to pay for his borrowed capital. But it is also interesting to see that the risk premium quite obviously increases in a recession, and furthermore, the volatility of interest rates increased in the 1980s. We will come back to these points.

Long-term monthly averages/weekly averages

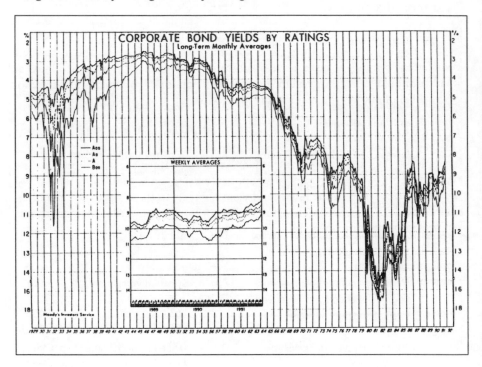

4.4 Market value: dependency on general interest rates

As with credit-worthiness, general interest rates cannot be contractually fixed. But an economy's interest rate trend has an extraordinarily important influence on the market value of a bond and in recent years this has shown relatively high volatility. This influence seems intuitively obvious. In determining the price of bonds, it is quite easy to understand that as the general interest rate level increases, a bond price decreases, because future payments will be discounted more heavily. In exactly the same way, bond prices will be expected to rise alongside falling interest rates because future payments are discounted less. But, the strength of the interest rate induced price changes again crucially depends on a number of bond-specific properties such as time to maturity, or coupon value. It is therefore important to understand this connection, because it gives a clear indication of which categories of bonds an investor should prefer to invest in, given certain opinions about the future direction of the level of market interest rates in an economy.

In order to give an overview of the effects of the various parameters, the price changes of four bonds with different properties are examined as a simple practical example. A market interest rate of 8% for all maturities is assumed, a final repayment of 100 and four different coupon interest rates. The following table shows the calculated prices of the bonds and what happens to these prices as each of the important data (market interest rate, coupon, time to maturity, repayment) are entered into equation (2.2).

| Bond price based on: | Time to maturity | | |
Coupon	2	6	10
0	85.73	63.02	46.32
4	92.87	81.51	73.16
8	100	100	100
12	107.13	118.49	126.84

The table can be interpreted as follows: The further away the coupon interest rate is from the general market interest rate (of 8%), and the longer the time to maturity, the more the bond's value deviates from 100.

We can also evaluate the price changes which occur if we assume interest rate changes of +/-2 and +/-4 percentage points respectively. The absolute and relative changes of the market price are given in the following table. ΔPV represents the absolute price change and $\Delta PV/PV$ represents the price change as a percentage of the respective market price.

Δ in % points	Coupon	Absolute and relative market value changes for ...					
		n = 2		n = 6		n = 10	
		Δ PV	Δ PV/PV	Δ PV	Δ PV/PV	Δ PV	Δ PV/PV
-4	0	+6.72	+7.84%	+16.01	+25.41%	+21.24	+45.85%
	4	+7.13	+7.68%	+18.49	+22.69%	+26.84	+36.69%
	8	+7.54	+7.54%	+20.97	+20.97%	+32.44	+32.44%
	12	+7.96	+7.43%	+23.45	+19.79%	+38.05	+30.00%
-2	0	+3.27	+3.81%	+7.48	+11.87%	+9.52	+20.55%
	4	+3.47	+3.73%	+8.66	+10.62%	+12.12	+16.57%
	8	+3.67	+3.67%	+9.83	+9.83%	+14.72	+14.72%
	12	+3.87	+3.61%	+11.01	+9.29%	+17.32	+13.66%
+2	0	-3.09	-3.60%	-6.57	-10.43%	-7.77	-16.76%
	4	-3.28	-3.53%	-7.64	-9.37%	-10.03	-13.71%
	8	-3.47	-3.47%	-8.71	-8.71%	-12.29	-12.29%
	12	-3.66	-3.42%	-9.78	-8.25%	-14.55	-11.47%
+4	0	-6.01	-7.02%	-12.35	-19.60%	-14.12	-30.49%
	4	-6.39	-6.88%	-14.40	-17.67%	-18.36	-25.10%
	8	-6.76	-6.76%	-16.45	-16.45%	-22.60	-22.60%
	12	-7.13	-6.66%	-18.49	-15.61%	-26.84	-21.16%

It can be seen from the table that the price changes increase as time to maturity lengthens and the coupon decreases.[1] The largest price change is therefore for a zero coupon bond with a time to maturity of 10 years (+45.85% if interest rates fall by 4 points or -30.49% if interest rates rise by 4 points). These findings are interesting because they point to **investment strategies for bond investors:** for instance, when interest rates are expected to fall, an investor should switch to 'long-term' bonds with relatively low coupons, whereas with rising interest rates, it is most advantageous to invest in bonds with fairly short times to maturity and high coupons in order to a) achieve a high yield potential and b) keep risks of capital (price) losses to a minimum. This is a strategy which may seem counter-intuitive to someone unfamiliar with financial markets.

As we know that the capital market yield, ie. the general level of interest rates, is determined mainly by the fundamental economic environment, expectations relating to the development of interest rate trends are mainly concerned with the development of the respective economic determinants. It therefore seems sensible to reflect on the economic models and hypotheses for determining interest rates.

---

[1]   The table is taken from UHLIR, H./STEINER, P.: 'Wertpapieranalyse', Physica Verlag, Heidelberg 1986.

5. Determination of the general level of interest rates

Economic theory indicates a number of influential factors which figure in most explanations of the general interest rate level and interest rate structure. We will discuss a few of these briefly. Factors include:

* the influence of government policy
* the influence of monetary policy
* the influence of market conditions/sentiment
* the influence of inflation
* the influence of foreign interest rates and exchange rate expectations

5.1 The influence of government policy

It is obvious, even from experience over the past few years alone, that government policies can considerably influence the capital market yield. Intuitively, the transmission mechanism seems relatively simple. It is reasonable to suppose that, ceteris paribus, the more additional finance the government requires from the capital markets instead of via increasing taxes, the higher the rate of interest it must offer, so that investors will be prepared to take up the additional government securities (the portfolio argument).

The 'ceteris paribus' condition includes the assumption of a constant volume of savings. This assumption has come under criticism within the theoretical literature: it is argued that the participants in the market would realise that debt financing is nothing but a delayed tax increase – ie. 'payment' falls due for the next generation. According to this argument, as investors supposedly do not want to pass such a tax increase on to following generations, they would rather increase savings (which will be inherited by future generations). Because of this savings increase, the demand for government bonds would increase and enable the debt financing to be neutral regarding interest rates. This theory is discussed in economics literature under the name of the Ricardian Equivalence Theorem.

Developments of the past 10 years, for example in the USA, give cause for some doubt over the validity of the Ricardo hypothesis, so that it seems sensible at least to assume that an excessive debt policy can have a certain impact on the development of interest rates.[1] We must also remember that other factors in the general economic

---

[1]   For an analysis of the theory of neutrality, compare GRASSEL, W.: 'Die These der Staatsschuldneutralität', Berlin 1984, or HERI, E.W.: 'Spielt es wirklich keine Rolle, wie die Staatsausgaben finanziert werden?', Geld & Währung, Series 3, 1987.

environment will undoubtedly affect the responsiveness of interest rates to increases in government deficit funding. For example, in weak economic conditions when private sector demand for funds is weak, the government may simply be filling a 'gap' in the market (ie. acting contra-cyclically as economic stabilisers such as unemployment benefits come into play). In contrast, increased government spending and thus borrowing would put more pressure on interest rates in a booming economy (creating the so-called 'crowding-out' effect by discouraging private sector borrowing for investment). The reaction of interest rates may not even be symmetric (or linear).

5.2 The influence of monetary policy

Monetary policy can influence the interest rate level through various channels. Firstly, the central bank influences the money market rate – ie. the short end of the interest rate spectrum – via its own activities in the money markets (eg. in the Federal Republic of Germany, via the regulation of rates at weekly repurchase agreements; in Switzerland, via foreign currency market interventions, etc.). A further possibility would be to attempt to change money supply by buying and selling long-term government bonds – not a very popular instrument in most countries.

Monetary policy is more likely to have medium-term, rather than short-term effects on the inflation rate, as well as inflation expectations. Although there may be exceptions in periods of structural change or financial market deregulation (as in the early 1980s), it is generally accepted that massive money supply growth above the real growth of an economy over a long period feeds inflation. Increasing inflation rates in such an environment are a signal which leads to changes in inflation expectations. Inflation expectations themselves are important parameters in determining the capital market yield. Expectations are difficult to control and once changed, may only become even more difficult to suppress, potentially creating a self-fulfilling spiral.

5.3 The influence of the business cycle

The influence of the business cycle on the interest rate level is all too often seen as clear cut: a trough in the business cycle is generally equated with low interest rates and vice versa. This relationship is, however, anything but clear.

Whilst low real growth or a recession undoubtedly leads to downward pressure on interest rates in credit markets, with savings deposit rates falling, on the contrary in capital markets, risk premiums may increase, so that a borrower of medium solvency suddenly has to offer higher rates than in 'good' market conditions to attract investors. This risk premium cycle seems to be unquestionably present, so that to examine the influence of the business cycle on the **general** interest rate level, a concrete definition of the respective interest rates is required. The following graph, taking the US as an example, illustrates how much the risk premium (ie. the **difference** in yields) of bonds for different qualities of debtors, fluctuates in changing market conditions (the shaded bands on the graph show periods of recession).

Risk premium cycles in the USA

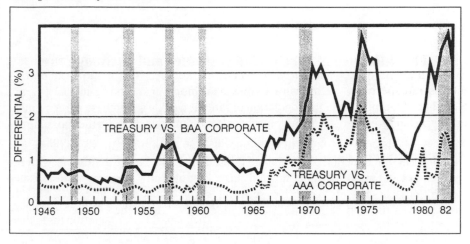

Source: Moody's

5.4 The influence of inflation

We have already alluded to the lasting influence of inflation on nominal capital market yields. We find, in fact, that countries with persistently high inflation records always and in every case have a higher interest rate level than countries with lower inflation rates, at least when free capital markets exist. The reason for this is relatively simple. Investors will not hold bonds purely because of the coupon payments, but chiefly because of what they can buy with the coupon and the later repayment. In other words, they will keep the bond because of its **real** value. They demand a coupon in which the expected inflation rate has already been 'included'. If 5% inflation is expected in the next year, then most investors, quite sensibly, would not be prepared to lend money at 5% today. In reality, if investors are not paid for providing capital in real terms, then a surplus supply of 'too low' yielding bonds tends to occur given lack of demand at such prices. This then pushes market prices down and the corresponding yields up, creating a new, higher interest rate environment and equilibrium.

However, we should briefly point out that there have been periods, even of several years duration, when interest rates have actually been below the rate of inflation in some countries, the late 1970s being one such period. In general, inflation expectations and/or real interest rate perceptions may be inaccurate, with investors misjudging the situation (savers may suffer from 'money illusion' or the 'appeal' of high nominal interest rates). This may result in a period of attrition, ie. higher real interest rates to compensate and reassure investors, which was indeed the case through much of the 1980s. In addition, there is a point which we touched on earlier: the vast OPEC money surplus which flooded the markets in the 1970s and seemed insensitive to the low real rates offered.

5.5 The influence of foreign interest rates and exchange rate expectations

Understandably, in a country with free capital markets and currency movements, domestic interest rates depend on interest rate developments abroad and exchange rate expectations, in addition to the points already mentioned above. In the simple theoretical model with fixed exchange rates, one would expect that bonds with the same risks and maturities at home and abroad should show the same yields. In such conditions, these assets are perfect substitutes, and it makes no difference whether bonds from the Federal Republic of Germany, the UK or the US are kept in the portfolio. If, for some reason, there were to be price differences, then investors would 'arbitrage' their positions so that the yields would balance out. If there were expectations of currency revaluations or devaluations in such a system due to some event or other, then the resulting movement in portfolios (investors seeking advantageous currency positions) would result in dramatic widening of interest rate differentials.The sharp fluctuations in French or Italian interest rates in the early 1980s at times of tension in the European currency system are an interesting example of this. Another, more recent, example was the increase in interest rates in Finland ahead of a devaluation of the Finnish mark in the fourth quarter of 1991. More dramatic still were the fluctuations in a number of European interest rates ahead of significant realignments of currencies in 1992.

With flexible exchange rates, revaluation and devaluation expectations have an essentially continuous role and therefore play a prominent part in setting domestic interest rate levels. In other words, a decoupling of interest rates is, theoretically, much more feasible than with fixed exchange rates. Additionally, it can be considered that the 'globalisation' of financial markets observed over the past few years, apart from making many investors' portfolios worldwide more international, has had an effect on domestic interest rate levels, with these reacting much more dramatically to changes in foreign interest rates and revaluation and devaluation expectations now than they did a decade ago.

A simple example of this: given lower interest rates in Switzerland than in the USA, an American investor will only favour SFr bonds over US bonds if he expects a Swiss Franc revaluation of at least the same magnitude as the difference in interest rates. If he does not do this, then he will stay away from the Swiss bond market. Under the circumstances, he could even sell his Swiss bonds and thus create upward pressure on Swiss capital market yields. The influence such factors can have in reality has been demonstrated in recent years in the US bond market, where the behaviour of Japanese investors has at times been influential in determining US yields.

Exchange rate expectations and foreign interest rates are therefore important parameters in determining domestic interest rate developments. Most of the countries with low interest rates can only decouple from an increasing interest rate trend in foreign countries in the medium term if expectations of a currency revaluation dominate the market (perhaps due to weakening inflation). Only then are investors prepared to hold lower interest rate investments.

The theoretical arguments put forward in this chapter concerning the macro-economics of interest rate determination were 'ceteris-paribus' analyses of the simplest form. But thanks to such simplicity, it was possible to evaluate a number of principles that can be found in practice in real-life markets. The last part of the chapter will describe general risk concepts for fixed income securities and a number of special types of bonds that do not fall within the framework of a simple 'straight bond' concept.

6. Interest rate and price risks of bonds

There are many ways of assessing the investment risk associated with purchasing bonds. Debtor risk, as described above, is one of these. Another is the **general price risk** which may be measured, for example, by historic volatility, a statistical concept which is not at all concerned with the reason for price changes. It is different again for **interest rate risk**, ie. the changes in market value according to changes in capital market yields. We showed in section 4.4 that an increase in interest rates, ceteris paribus, leads to a decrease in the price of a bond, and vice versa. We also showed in an example that the expected changes – the price risk – were dependent on the time left to maturity and coupon value. Here, we want to emphasise the 'and' part, especially as only a few years ago the general opinion was that the time left to maturity was the only criterion for determining the interest rate risk of a fixed interest position. In fact, we must also look specifically at the value of the coupon as has already been shown above. The relevant risk measurement is therefore no longer the (time left to) maturity, but the so-called **duration,** which is occasionally described as the average maturity of a bond. This not only takes into account the repayment amount, but also the coupon payment. We have seen in section 4.4 how market price changes can be calculated. The duration in this case gives us the same result in a rather elegant way.

We will show how the duration is calculated and how far it gives us a direct means of determining the size of the percentage change in the bond price against a one percentage change in the interest rate. Once we have this measurement, we will be able to assess the interest rate risk of a bond position.

We will start with a simple example. The duration – the average lifetime – of a bond with a time to maturity of 3 years and a 6% coupon can be calculated as follows (capital market yield for all maturities also assumed to be 6%):

Year	1	2	3	Σ
Payments	60	60	1060	1180
PV of payment	56.60	53.40	890	1000

$$D = \frac{56.6 \times 1 + 53.4 \times 2 + 890 \times 3}{1000} = 2.83 \text{ (years)}$$

From this calculation it emerges that we are indeed dealing with an average maturity, and indeed the average duration of the commitment of capital in relation to the respective present values.

The duration of the above investment – the average maturity of all coupon payments together with the capital repayment – is 2.83 years. Any early capital return (eg. in the form of higher coupon payments) would reduce the average duration of the investment. The later the respective capital returns, the lower their value would be, as there would be less interest and compound interest paid. With an increasing coupon value, the duration would be reduced, and vice versa.

The duration can be depicted in graphic form, imagining the cash values of the individual payments to be 'weights' on a 'scale'. We can then ask where would the 'balance' point be? For our example, it would look like this:

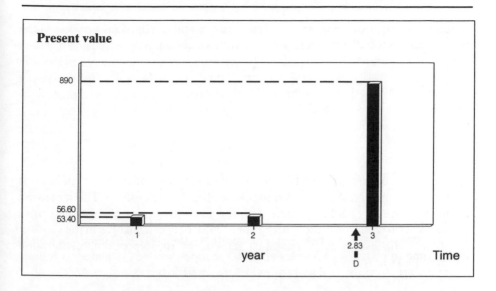

The respective bars indicate the present value of the payments within the three years and the arrow on the horizontal axis shows where 'balance would be achieved'. From the graph it becomes clear that the more the statistics (in the sense of present values of payments) are moved to the left, the 'shorter' the duration becomes. It also becomes clear that with a zero coupon bond, for which no interest payments fall due, the duration is equal to the maturity.

The general formula for calculating the duration is:

$$(2.4) \qquad D = \frac{\sum t . PV(t)}{\sum PV(t)}$$

Here, t represents the individual periods and PV(t) is the present value of the payments due within period t.

Alternatively, if we write down the present values and use the same terms as in the compound interest digression in section two[1], we obtain:

$$(2.5) \qquad D = \frac{\displaystyle\sum_{t=1}^{n} \frac{1}{(1+r)^{t}} \, C_t \times t}{\displaystyle\sum_{t=1}^{n} \frac{1}{(1+r)^{t}} \, C_t}$$

The duration concept is interesting because it can give us both a simplified interest rate risk measure and the interest rate potential of a bond position. This means we no longer have to calculate a table with the respective price changes and price increases, as in section 4.4. Indeed, the connection between changes in the value of bonds and changes in market interest rates using the (approximate) duration measure looks as follows:

$$(2.6) \qquad \begin{array}{l}\text{Change in value} \\ \text{of a bond}\end{array} = \frac{\text{Duration x Change in market interest rates (\%)}}{(1 + \text{previous interest rate})}$$

In our original example, we calculated a duration of 2.83. We assumed a time to maturity of 3 years, a coupon of 6% and also a market interest rate of 6%.

If the market interest rate increases from 6% to 7%, then the price of the bond will change by

$$\frac{-2.83 \times 1}{1.06} = -2.62\%$$

ie. it falls by 2.62%

---

[1] From this definition, it can also be seen that the duration of zero coupon bonds is equal to the maturity n, as zero coupon bonds by definition pay out only at the end of the investment, by implication including all interest and compound interest in the final repayment sum. This is therefore equivalent to there being only one C, which is paid after n periods, ie.

$$D = \frac{\dfrac{C_n \cdot n}{(1+r)^{n}}}{\dfrac{C_n}{(1+r)^{n}}} = \frac{C_n \cdot n}{C_n} = n. \quad \text{q.e.d.}$$

Now, what does the duration of the City of Yokohama bonds, already used as an example several times, look like, and how does the price change if the capital market yield rises by one percentage point? In order to answer these questions, we will assume a time to maturity of 8 years (in other words we will start the calculation from 10 December 1989), a capital market yield as for similar bonds of 7% and a denomination of SFr 100,000. The table needed for the calculation looks like this:

Years (t)	Payment	Present value (PV (t))	t x PV(t)
1	5,000	4,673	4,673
2	5,000	4,367	8,734
3	5,000	4,081	12,243
4	5,000	3,814	15,256
5	5,000	3,565	17,825
6	5,000	3,332	19,992
7	5,000	3,114	21,798
8	105,000	61,110	488,880
		88,056	**589,401**

According to equation (2.4) the duration of our CoY bonds is therefore

$$D = \frac{589401}{88056} = 6.69 \text{ years}$$

And the expected change in value for a one percentage point increase in capital market yield is

$$\text{Market price change} = \frac{-6.69 \times 1}{1.07} = -6.25\%$$

Therefore, an investor would lose 6.25% on the CoY bond in December 1989, if the capital market interest rate were to rise by a further one percentage point.

Let us be very pragmatic and compare these figures with what actually happened to the CoY bond (remembering again the first graph in which the value of the CoY bonds was set against Swiss market yields). We would expect that if the duration had been similar in December 1987, the approximate one and a half percentage point increase in interest rates over the following 18 months would have caused a price decrease of 9.4%. In fact, the price did fall by some 10%, from about 104 to around 94. Even though we have calculated very generously and 'very approximately', we have actually come quite close to the 'correct', 'real' result; we therefore find quite acceptable the estimate of the interest rate risk of our CoY bonds using the duration concept.

All these calculations are only very approximate and are only valid for small changes in interest rates, and they assume a flat interest rate structure. In this respect, the above considerations are rather inexact. This is to do with the fact that the correlation between the value of a bond and market interest rates is not strictly linear, but convex, and we are making a very brave assumption of a flat interest rate structure. For large (expected) interest rate changes, and in managing large bond portfolios, it makes sense to take these problems into consideration. However, it would be beyond the scope of this book to introduce methods for treating these in more detail.[1]

The previous analysis makes it clear that duration as a measurement of risk records the interest rate risk of bonds and bond portfolios exclusively. In many cases – especially if one argues in the context of a portfolio – it will be necessary to assume risk in the sense of general volatility. Here, statistical concepts such as Variance and Standard Deviation, amongst others, become relevant. We will discuss such concepts in more detail when we tackle issues relating to portfolio theory.

7. Innovations in bond markets

In the discussions so far, we have used almost exclusively examples of 'straight bonds', although it was initially mentioned that 'straight bonds' in today's capital markets are actually becoming rare. The City of Yokohama bond that we have already used on many occasions is not precisely a classic 'straight bond', because if we read the quotation advertisement carefully, we will find that the issuer has the right, under certain conditions, to pay back the loan earlier, ie. he has a call option (favourable to the issuer). This option, of course, has a value which could mean that, given efficient pricing, the yield of this bond might be higher, or must be higher, than the yield of bonds without this option attached.

Over the past few years, issuing houses have approached the markets with a vast number of new and varied bond contracts. It would go well beyond the frame of this introduction if we were to explain all these new tools and discuss their pricing in more

---

[1]   For this, compare with (for example) GABRIEL HAWAWINI, Controlling the Interest-Rate Risk of Bonds. An Introduction to Duration Analysis and Immunization Strategies', Finanzmarkt und Portfolio-management, Jg. 1 Nr. 4, p.8-18.

detail. But it seems sensible to explain some of these innovations briefly. With regard to pricing, it is sufficient to point out that for all instruments, the basic principle remains that the price firstly equals the present value of all (expected) future payments. According to the form of the loan and the instruments themselves, the payments will often become dependent on the development of certain other financial market prices. Thus, probability assumptions concerning various forms of price changes – volatility in the broadest sense – play a much more important role.

7.1 Zero-coupon bonds

Zero-coupon bonds (often called nil-coupon bonds) are bonds for which no continuous interest is paid. We have already mentioned zero coupon bonds in the above explanation of the duration measure. We stated then that the duration of zero coupon bonds is equal to their maturity. In other words, for a given maturity, the zero coupon bond is the investment instrument with the greatest interest risk. If one likes to think in extremes, zero coupon bonds seem to be the best investment choice under an assumption of falling interest rates, but one better avoided in the opposite case.

The 'yield' of zero coupon bonds results from the difference between issue price and the discounted repayment sum. Such a bond is a 'discount' paper for which final repayment already includes all interest and compound interest to maturity.

In principle, it is slightly exaggerated to talk about the concept of zero coupon bonds as a 'new' idea because, in the USA, these have already been in operation for decades with Treasury Bills, Commercial Paper or Bankers' Acceptances, which are all traded on this discount basis. However, longer maturities first came into use in 1981 (eg. J.C. Penney, 1981-2021), and with this, the possibility of covering long-term obligations earlier than expected.

It has already been pointed out that the use of compound interest calculations in bond analysis (eg. yield to maturity) can lead to false or misleading appraisals, for example, because coupon payments are not (cannot be) invested at the expected interest rates used in the calculations. Consequently, the answer may be the zero coupon bond. As a discount paper, the price of these bonds implies a systematic reinvestment. In this sense, it solves the problem of reinvestment already on purchase. But even here, a 'price' has to be paid in the form of higher price risks on the bonds as discussed above.

On the following page, we reproduced the application offer of the Caisse Nationale de Crédit Agricole Zero-Coupon-Bonds issued in Autumn 1990. Maturity was 4.4 years and the issue price was 70.495%. The amount paid in 1990 was $70,495 and that to be received in 1995 (if not repaid earlier) was fixed at $100,000. The resulting yield on expiry is:

$$(1.7) \qquad R = \sqrt[n]{\frac{T}{PV}} - 1 = \sqrt[4,4]{\frac{100,000}{70,495}} - 1 = 8.3\%$$

In times of high interest rates, the demand for zero coupon bonds is particularly high. Occasionally, brokers have created so-called synthetic zero coupon bonds, for example, by buying in Treasury bonds, separating the expected coupons from the bonds and trading them separately. From this separation, 'many little zero coupons' with different maturities can be produced. CATS (Certificate of Accrual on Treasury Securities, from Salomon Brothers), LIONs (Lehman Investments Opportunity Notes, from Lehman Brothers), STRIPs (Separate Trading of Registered Interest and Principal of Securities, issued by the US Treasury itself) or ZEBRAs (Zero Coupon Euro-Sterling Bearer of Registered Accruing Securities, issued by investment houses in London), are just some of these creations.

Caisse Nationale de Crédit Agricole

US$ 120,000,000

Zero Coupon Notes due 1995

Issue Price: 70.495 per cent

The US$ 120,000,000 Zero Coupon Notes due 1995 (the 'Notes') of Caisse Nationale de Crédit Agricole ('CNCA') will be issued outside France in bearer form in the denomination of US$ 1,000,000 each.

The Notes will mature on 15 March 1995 and are not redeemable prior to maturity, except that all, but not some only, of the Notes may, and in some circumstances shall, be redeemed at their redemption amount if certain French taxes are imposed on payments on the Notes, as set out under 'Terms and Conditions of the Notes – Redemption and Purchase'.

Application has been made to list the Notes on the Luxembourg Stock Exchange.

Selling restrictions have been imposed on offers and sales of the Notes and on distribution of documents relating thereto, including in the United States, in the Republic of France and in the United Kingdom, see 'Subscription and Sale'.

A temporary certificate in respect of the Notes (the 'Temporary Certificate') will initially be deposited with a common depositary for Euroclear and CEDEL SA on or about 15 October 1990. The Temporary Certificate will be exchangeable for Notes in definitive form on or after a date which is expected to be 26 November 1990, and in any event not later than 14 January 1991.

Sanwa International Plc

       Crédit Agricole

             New Japan Securities Europe Limited

                    Sanwa Bank (Deutschland) AG

Dated: 9 October 1990

US$ 400,000,000

Subordinated Undated Variable Rate Notes

Santander Financial Issuances Limited
(Incorporated in the Cayman Islands with limited liability)

with payment of interest subject to the profits of and
secured by a subordinated deposit with

Banco de Santander, S.A. de Crédito

(Incorporated in Spain with limited liability)

Interest on the Notes will be payable quarterly in arrear on 16 March, 16 June, 16 September and 16 December in each year (subject as provided herein), with the first payment in September 1990. Interest will be payable at a rate per annum equal to the aggregate of the relevant margin and three month US dollar LIBOR (except that the rate for the first Interest Period will be by reference to two month US dollar LIBOR). See 'Description of the Notes – Interest'.

The margin will be reset in respect of each Interest Period. If the new margin is less than a certain percentage, Noteholders may, subject as provided in 'Description of the Notes – Redemption and Purchase', require Salomon Brothers International Limited, as Remarketing Underwriter, to purchase such Notes at their principal amount.

Payment of interest will be deferred if the non-consolidated accounts of Banco de Santander, SA de Crédito (the 'Bank') do not show a profit.

The Notes are undated and have no final maturity. All or some of the Notes may be redeemed at the option of Santander Financial Issuances Limited (the 'Issuer') at their principal amount on any Interest payment Date falling in or after September 1995.

Issue price 100 per cent

The obligations of the Issuer in respect of the Notes will be subordinated to all unsubordinated payment obligations of the Issuer, as described in 'Description of the Notes – Status, Subordination and Deposit Arrangements'. The Notes will be secured by an assignment of the Issuer's rights in respect of a subordinated deposit made with the Bank.

The Notes will be represented by a temporary Global Note, without interest coupons, which is expected to be deposited with a common depositary from Morgan Guaranty Trust Company of New York, Brussels office, as operator of the Euroclear system ('Euroclear') and CEDEL S.A. ('CEDEL') on or about 16 July 1990 (the 'Closing Date'). The temporary Global Note will be exchanged for a further Global Note ont he Exchange Date (as defined in 'Description of the Notes – Form, Denomination and Transfer'). Save in certain limited circumstances or upon request by a Noteholder, Notes in definitive form will be issued in exchange for the Global Note.

Application has been made to the Council of The International Stock Exchange fo the United Kingdom and the Republic of Ireland Limited ('The Stock Exchange') for the Notes to be admitted to the Official List. Copies of this document which constitutes the listing particulars required by the listing rules made under Section 142 of the Financial Services Act 1986 have been delivered to the Registrar of Companies in England and Wales as required by Section 149 of the Financial Services Act 1986.

The Notes have not been and will not be registered under the US Securities Act of 1933 and are subject to US tax law requirements. Subject to certain exceptions, Notes may not be offered, sold or delivered within the United States or to US persons.

7.2 Floating rate notes

A floating rate note (FRN) is a loan with a non-fixed coupon. The interest provisions of such a bond are as a rule governed by a certain basic (market) interest rate (for example LIBOR, the rate at which banks based in London lend each other short-term money), which serves as a reference measure for regularly fixing new rates for the note.

We have already met 'Floaters' in the international finance chart in the introduction. They were introduced as a special category which became particularly popular with issuers when interest rates were coming down between 1982 and 1986. From 1987, as interest rates tended to turn around again, such instruments have become less significant.

As an example of such a 'floater', we show the quotation advertisement for the undated Banco de Santander bonds. The interest rate coupon for this bond is adjusted to three month US dollar LIBOR every 3 months. In this example, the premium to LIBOR actually paid is linked to the profitability of the issuer, with the investor offered the opportunity to redeem the bonds should profitability not achieve a certain level. But no interest will be paid if the issuer does not show a profit.

Because the variable for the pricing of a floating rate note is, in principle, the interest rate, and not the present value, the stockmarket value of such a bond is, as a rule, around par value. Accordingly, a floating rate note has more or less the characteristics of a continuously self-renewing money market (or savings deposit) investment for the investor.

7.3 Convertible bonds

With convertible bonds, an investor buys a fixed interest rate security of a certain nominal value, which, on expiry, will pay a pre-determined repayment sum – ie. a 'straight bond' in the broadest sense. At the same time, however, the investor also receives the right (the 'option') to exchange the paper during the so-called conversion period, at a fixed price (conversion price), for another instrument, usually a share or a participation certificate for the company concerned. If during the conversion period the investor decides to convert, then the bonds are, in effect, cancelled, the debtor replaces the borrowed capital by his own capital and the investor finds himself owning the alternative instrument (shares) in exchange. The price paid by an investor for this extra 'right' is a lower coupon compared with ordinary bonds. In principle, this is nothing other than the premium for a 'call' option (buying right) on the corresponding alternative instrument (eg. share).

US$ 100,000,000

LONRHO

Lonrho Finance Public Limited Company
(Incorporated in England under the Companies Acts 1948 to 1981)

$4^{3}/_{4}$ per cent Convertible Guaranteed Bonds Due 2001

Convertible into ordinary shares of, and
unconditionally and irrevocably guaranteed by,

Lonrho Public Limited Company
(Incorporated in England under the Companies (Consolidation) Act, 1908)

The issue price of the Bonds is 100 per cent of their principal amount, plus accrued interest, if any. Interest in respect of the Bonds will accrue from 30 April 1986 and will be payable annually in arrear on 30 April. Payments of principal, premium (if any) and interest in respect of the Bonds will be made without deduction for or on account of United Kingdom taxes to the extent set out herein. The Bonds will mature on 30 April 2001, unless previously converted, redeemed or purchased and cancelled as set out herein.

Each Bond will be convertible at the holder's option on or after 6 May 1986 and up to and including 20 April 2001 into ordinary shares of Lonrho Public Limited Company ('Lonrho' or the 'Guarantor') at an initial conversion price, which is subject to adjustment in certain events set out herein, of 272.4p per ordinary share (with a fixed rate of exchange applicable on conversion of $1.4684 = £1). This conversion price has been established by reference to the share price adjusted to reflect the one-for-ten bonus issue of ordinary shares referred to under 'Information Concerning the Share Capital of Lonrho' below (the 'Bonus Issue') and no further adjustment will be made for the Bonus Issue. On 16 April 1986, the closing middle market quotation of the ordinary shares of Lonrho on The Stock Exchange of the United Kingdom and the Republic of Ireland ('The Stock Exchange') was 265p per ordinary share. This price takes into account the entitlement to the Bonus Issue. With effect from 28 April 1986, the ordinary shares are expected to be dealt in without entitlement to the Bonus Issue.

Application has been made to the Council of The Stock Exchange for the Bonds to be admitted to the Official List. A copy of this Prospectus, which comprises the listing particulars required by The Stock Exchange (Listing) Regulations 1984, has been delivered to the Registrar of Companies in England and Wales in Accordance with Regulation 7(5) thereof.

The Bonds will be represented initially by a temporary global bond (the 'Global Bond') which will be deposited with a common depositary for Euro-clear and CEDEL S.A. on or about 30 April 1986 and which will be exchangeable for definitive Bonds in bearer form not earlier than 90 days after completion of the distribution of the Bonds.

Credit Suisse First Boston Limited	**Nomura International Limited**
Arab Banking Corporation (B.S.C.)	**Berliner Handels- und Frankfurter Bank**
Credit Lyonnais	**Deutsche Bank Capital Markets Limited**
Generale Bank	**Kredietbank N.V.**
Lloyds Merchant Bank Limited	**Merrill Lynch International & Co.**
Standard Chartered Merchant Bank Limited	**Swiss Bank Corporation International Limited**

The date of this Prospectus is 17 April 1986

On the previous and following pages examples of convertible bonds are given. The first is the $4^3/_4$% 1986 - 2001 Lonrho issue. The second example is the (German language) quotation advertisement of the $2^1/_2$% 1989-1995 Fuchs Petrolub AG convertible bonds. This paper gives the right to exchange bonds of SFr 3,000 nominal value for Fuchs Petrolub bearer shares. The conversion period is over the total maturity of the bonds, conversion price is in principle SFr 550.

The speciality of the Fuchs Petrolub convertible is that the investor also has the option, under certain conditions, to demand repayment in May 1993 (this is, in effect, a put, ie. sell option).

The difference between the price of the share on the stockmarket and the price paid for the share if bought via convertible bonds is called the conversion premium. As the Fuchs Petrolub bearer share was priced at around SFr 3,000 at the end of October 1989, this equalled approximately the conversion price. The size of the conversion premium naturally influences the pricing of the convertible bonds and also the question of whether such an instrument has more the characteristics of a share or a bond (clearly it is a hybrid!). At a very high conversion premium, the yield of convertible bonds is not too far away from the yield of 'straight bonds', and an investor practically has a bond in his portfolio. The higher the conversion premium, and the lower the exchange potential versus the market prices of the shares, the lower the value of the exchange option. Accordingly, convertible bonds for which a profitable exchange into shares (or other instruments) up to maturity does not seem feasible, must be judged by practically the same criteria as those used for 'straight bonds'. In effect, the option to convert in this extremely unfavourable situation is akin to a lottery ticket with a very small probability of producing a return for the investor.

On the other hand, for convertible bonds with very low or even negative conversion premiums, an investor could almost be said to hold shares in his portfolio. It would accordingly be legitimate to consider buying the shares themselves instead of the convertibles. A decision in favour of the convertible would probably only be made if the convertible were to show a significantly higher yield than the shares themselves (for the time being, we are omitting the evaluation of the benefits of participation rights granted by shares). Alternatively, the relative attraction of the convertibles may be that dividends are treated differently from interest payments in some way, for example for tax purposes, or because of perceived risk of dividend volatility, especially during periods of general economic weakness or recession.

For a more detailed/technical treatment of convertibles, we refer the reader to specialised guides [1].

---

[1] For example ZUBULAKE, L.A.: 'The Complete Guide to Convertible Securities Worldwide', John Wiley.

7.4 Dual currency bonds

Dual currency bonds (DCB) and so-called Foreign Interest Payment Securities (FIPS) are fixed-interest instruments which contain in addition to the usual coupon and repayment specifications special features concerning exchange rates. For DCBs, issue of title and interest payments are made in a different currency to the repayment sum. Repayment is made most commonly in the currency of the issuer, while issue and interest payments are made in the currency of a country with low interest rates – typically the currency has often been the Yen or SFr. Accordingly, such an instrument has the characteristics of a 'hybrid', because in addition to the interest rate risks, the investor is also burdened with exchange rate risks which must be evaluated. Therefore, the coupon of a US$/SFr DCB, for example, will be somewhere between the coupon of foreign bonds in SFr of identical risk, and the respective dollar bonds. Furthermore, a repayment price defined in a foreign currency on issue is offered which is typically above (often well above) the issue price.

7.5 Warrants

Particularly because of the general existence of 'bullish' stockmarkets through the 1980s, at least prior to the 1987 crash, bonds with warrants (or option bonds) became a favourite finance and investment instrument. One of their features is that they are not all that different to the convertibles described above. However, in this case, a bond is not exchanged for an alternative instrument such as a share, but is combined with a separable option note, the so-called warrant, which provides the holder with the right to acquire an alternative instrument (ordinary shares, participation certificates or any other more or less marketable product) for a certain price (exercise price) from a specified date. An investor not only purchases a bond, but also an option at the same time. If the investor uses the option (right), or if it is sold separately, the bonds continue to exist until maturity (as a rule, as 'straight bonds)', however, it is then said that the bond is traded ex-option. It is clear, that as investments, options do not come free of charge. The 'price' paid – besides the option exercise price – is a lower coupon which, depending on the bullishness of the assumptions used in determining the price of the offered instrument, can be fixed very low indeed. An impressive example of how low the coupon can be has been seen in the Japanese warrant market, which was extraordinarily active for a long time during the period of the Japanese stockmarket's particularly spectacular rise in the 1980s.

An example of an option bond can be found below where there is a quotation advertisement for the $5^7/_8$% bonds with warrants of Nestlé 1991 - 1998. The features of these securities are as follows: Each of the $10,000 bonds has 90 warrants attached and for each 60 warrants held an investor has the right to buy one Nestlé (registered) share at a price of SFr 9,200 (subject to stated conditions) up to 30 November 1994.

With option bonds, one actually purchases two (separate) instruments, correspondingly there are three market valuations to consider:

- Bonds cum option
- Bonds ex option
- Option certificates (warrants) alone

The value of the bonds cum is thus composed of the value of the bond (ex) itself together with the value of the option certificate (warrant). Pricing and risk analysis of the bond ex is handled according to the principles seen above when discussing 'straight bonds'. To evaluate the warrants themselves, special statistical procedures for pricing options are applied (the most well-known being based on the Black-Scholes model). These procedures need to take into account the price behaviour of the instrument (eg. share) being offered, particularly its volatility, a concept we will discuss in the following chapter on equity analysis.

We have introduced a number of bonds for which pricing can no longer be done solely by means of a simple compound interest calculation. To discuss pricing for such varied investment instruments in more detail would take this introduction too far. Readers interested in further details are therefore directed to the respective financial market literature.[1]

In this chapter we have tried to increase the understanding of general questions of price setting for fixed interest investment instruments, as well as offering some insight into various problems, including the fact that bonds are perhaps not always as risk-free as they may appear from the seemingly fixed parameters offered. The bonds chapter is the most voluminous in this book. In light of the importance of fixed interest investments in most savings plans/portfolios, and given the knowledge that bond analysis still suffers something of a wallflower existence with many investors, this priority seems justified.

---

[1]   For example: PHILIPS, G.: 'Japanese Warrant Markets', Macmillan, for a more detailed treatment of warrants; WONG, M.A.: 'Trading and Investing in Bond Options', John Wiley, for a specific treatment of the US bond options market; HULL, J.: 'Options, Futures and other Derivative Securities', Woodhead Faulkner, for detailed coverage of valuation techniques; THOMSETT, M.C.: 'Getting Started in Options', John Wiley, or RITCHKEN, P.H.: 'Options', Harper Collins, or BOOKSTABER, R.M.: 'Option Pricing and Investment Strategies', Probus, for general introductory treatments of options and their use. Further information on bond market strategies can be found in FABOZZI, F.J.: 'Bond Markets Analysis and Strategies', Woodhead Faulkner, or THOMSETT, M.C.: 'Getting Started in Bonds', John Wiley.

FUCHS PETROLUB AG
Frauenfeld TG (Schweiz)

2% Wandelanleihe 1989095 von Fr. 30 000 000

Wichtigste Bedingungen

Zweck: Finanzierung des weiteren Ausbaus des Beteiligungsportefeuillles

Inhabertitel: von Fr. 3000 und Fr. 90 000 Nennwert

Verzinsung: 2%

Laufzeit: bis längstens 30. Juni 1995

Wandelrecht: Obligationen von je Fr. 3000 Nennwert können ab 3. November 1989 bis zur Fälligkeit bzw. bis zum vorzeitigen Rückzahlungstermin der Anleihe spesenfrei in 1 Inhaberaktie von Fr. 1000 Nennwert der Fuchs Petrolub AG gewandelt werden.

Wandelpreis: Fr. 3550 – je 1 Inhaberaktie. Die Differenz zwischen dem Wandelpreis und dem Nennwert der Obligation ist anlässlich der Wandlung in bar einzuzahlen bzw. wird anlässlich der Wandlung in bar ausbezahlt, sofern der Wandelpreis aufgrund des Verwässerungsschutzes auf unter Fr. 3000 ermässigt wird.

Emissionspreis: 100%

Zeichnungsfrist: vom 16. bis 20. Oktober 1989, mittags

Liberierung: 3. November 1989

Kotierung: wird an der Börse von Zürich beantragt

Put-Option: des Investors: Die Obligationäre haben das Recht, innerhalb der Frist vom 1. Mai bis zum 31. Mai 1993 die Rückzahlung ihrer Obligation zu 110.25% des Nennwertes, zuzüglich aufgelaufener Zinsen, auf den 30. Juni 1993 zu verlangen. Bei Geltendmachung der Put-Option nach rund 3²/₃ Jahren Laufzeit beträgt die Rendite für die Obligationäre 4.64%. Die Put-Prämie von 10.25% unterliegt der eidgenössischen Verrechnungssteuer von 35%.

Dividendenberechtigung: für das Geschäftsjahr, in welchem das Wandelrecht ausgeübt wird.

Verwässerungsschutz: bei Kapitaltransaktionen mit Bezugsrecht durch Reduktion des Wandelpreises.

Die vollständigen Anleihebedingungen sind auf der Rückseite aufgeführt.

Ein Kotierungsinserat wird am 16. Oktober 1989 in der <Neuen Zürcher Zeitung> veröffentlicht. Für weitere Angaben über die Fuchs Petrolub AG, Frauenfeld, verweisen wir auf den Prospekt über die Kapitalerhöhung 1989, der bei den Banken eingesehen werden kann.

Zeichnungsangebot

Die unterzeichneten Banken haben die obenbeschriebene Anleihe von Fr. 30 000 000 fest übernommen und legen sie in der Zeit vom **16. bis 20. Oktober 1989**, mittags, zu den folgenden Bedingungen zur öffentlichen Zeichnung auf:

1. Der **Emissionspreis** beträgt 100%.

2. **Zeichnungen** werden spesenfrei durch die schweizerischen Geschäftsstellen der unterzeichneten Banken entgegengenommen.

3. **Zuteilung** nach Schluss der Zeichnungsfrist. Wenn die Zeichnungen den verfügbaren Anleihebetrag übersteigen, sind die Banken berechtigt, bei der Zuteilung Kürzungen vorzunehmen.

4. **Liberierung** der zugeteilten Titel hat auf den 3. November 1989 zu erfolgen.

5. Die **Lieferung** der Titel erfolgt so bald als möglich.

Schweizerische Kreditanstalt

Schweizerische Bankgesellschaft
Deutsche Bank (Schweiz) AG
Südwestdeutsche Landesbank (Schweiz) AG

Schweizerischer Bankverein
Dresdner Bank (Schweiz) AG

Valoren-Nummern:	
Anleihe	106,943
Inhaberaktie	176,996

US$ 200,000,000

Nestlé Holdings, Inc.

(Incorporated in the State of Delaware with limited liability)

5$^7/_8$ per cent Bonds Due 1998

with Warrants issued by Nestlé's Holdings Limited, Nassau
to acquire an aggregate of 30,000 Registered Shares of

Nestlé S.A.

(Incorporated in Switzerland with limited liability)

Offering Price of the Bonds with Warrants:
100 per cent of the principal amount of the Bonds

Interest on the 5$^7/_8$ per cent Bonds due 1998 (the 'Bonds') is payable annually in arrears on 19 June of each year commencing 19 June 1992. Payments on the Bonds will be made without deduction for United States withholding taxes, to the extent described under 'Description of the Bonds of the Company – Payment of Additional Amounts'.

Each definitive US$ 10,000 Bond will be issued with 90 warrants issued by Nestlé's Holdings Limited. The Holder of 60 Warrants will be entitled to acquire one Registered Share of Nestlé S.A. at a price of SFr 9,200, subject to adjustment as described under 'Description of the Warrants of NHL – Adjustment of Exercise Price'. Definitive Warrants will be exercisable on or after 30 July 1991 until 30 November 1994, upon presentation of certificates of exercise outside the United States as described under 'Description of the Warrants of NHL – Rights to Acquire Shares'.

Application has been made to list the Bonds with Warrants, the Bonds and the Warrants on the Luxembourg Stock Exchange.

The Bonds and the Warrants (together, the 'Securities') will initially be represented by a temporary Global Bond and a temporary Global Warrant, both of which will be deposited with a common depositary for CEDEL S.A. ('CEDEL') and Morgan Guaranty Trust Company of New York, Brussels office, as operator of the Euroclear System ('Euroclear'), on or about 19 June 1991. The temporary Global Bond will be exchangeable for definitive Bonds in bearer form not earlier than 40 days after delivery of and payment for the temporary Global bond, and upon presentation of certificates of non-US beneficial ownership as set forth in the Fiscal Agency Agreement as described under 'Description of the Bonds of the Company – Form and Denomination'. Upon presentation of similar certificates, the temporary Global Warrant will be exchangeable for definitive Warrants not earlier than 30 July 1991 as described under 'Description of the Warrants of NHL – Form and Transfer'.

UBS Phillips & Drew Securities Limited

Credit Suisse First Boston Limited	**Swiss Bank Corporation**
Bankers Trust International Limited	**Banque Bruxelles Lambert S.A.**
Citicorp Investment Bank Limited	**Credit Lyonnais Securities**
Deutsche Bank Capital Markets Limited	**Girozentrale und Bank der österreichischen Sparkassen**
JP Morgan Securities Ltd	**Paribas Capital Markets Group**
Julius Baer International Limited	**BSI-Banca della Svizzera Italiana**
Coutts & Co, AG	**Leu Securities Limited**
Swiss Cantobank Securities Limited	**Swiss Volksbank**

The date of this Offering Circular is 7 June 1991

Chapter 3

Equities

1. Introduction and definition

An equity holder, ie. the holder of share certificates relating to a company and its share capital, is a part owner of the said company, according to the proportion of shares held. Shares are therefore 'membership right securities', which comprise rights to assets and certain 'membership'. Basically, the membership gives the right to participate in the Annual General Meeting, together with voting and election rights for all matters arising from the Meeting. The rights to assets consist of part-entitlement to the proceeds in the possible event of a liquidation, the right to purchase new shares on issue, and a yield in the form of a dividend (although this payment may have no, or only partial, guarantee).

From this definition, the basic difference between equities and bonds is clear. While the shareholder owns rights to 'membership' and assets, the bondholder only has claims to certain monetary compensations. The shareholder makes available share capital, the bondholder external funds; and the shareholder only has limited rights to a dividend payment (yield), while the bondholder has rights to the interest payment as fixed in the contract, as well as final repayment. In the case of liquidation of a company, there are also differences in priorities and treatment for bond versus shareholders which favour the former. These differences cannot, of course, be without influence on pricing.

In practice, there are many different types of shares, the differences being shown in their inherent rights. Variations in these rights exist both across countries and within countries, a point we can illustrate by taking the example of Switzerland, where a typical quoted company has three share classes, Registered, Bearer and Participation Certificates.

Classes of shares

The example of Switzerland

The two most important categories of shares are Bearer Shares and Registered Shares. **Bearer Shares** are owned by the holder at any point in time ('whoever has them, owns them'), and they are transferable without restrictions. In contrast, the **Registered Shares** are registered in the name of the respective owners. To transfer them, the owner needs an 'endorsement' (noting any change of hands on the reverse side of the document, 'in dossa' = on the back), together with a new entry on the company's share register. In principle, it is also possible to register the shares as transferable only with the issuer's consent, giving the company the power to object to entry on the share register according to the statutes. In practice, this power has been seen as increasingly controversial and there is pressure to change such systems.

As a rule, the claim to shareholders' rights is in proportion to the nominal value of the shares held. In some cases, however, the creation of 'voting right shares' has enabled a certain circle of shareholders, without capital majority, to gain a voting majority. This has been achieved by the distribution of a vote to 'voting right shares' regardless of the nominal value, whilst providing the rights to assets with respect to the nominal value. The exact opposite can be achieved by issuing **Preference Shares,** which are usually given certain 'preferential' (guaranteed) dividend rights in order to, for example, provide founder members with adequate compensation and/or provide a better guarantee of income (via the dividend) and repayment in the event of liquidation of the company. **Genussscheine** (Participation Certificates, or PCs in the common abbreviation) are similar to preference shares. These are 'company rights participation certificates' containing only rights to assets with no membership rights. Furthermore, since 1963, the 'Participation Certificate' has been used as a special type of Genussschein to provide capital. For a company, the advantage of financing by issuing Participation Certificates lies in the unchanged structure of the voting rights.

Switzerland is not the only country in which companies issue a variety of types of share, or rather, shares with different types of rights attached. The 'voting' versus 'non-voting' classification is also common in Scandinavia although not in major equity markets such as the US or, in Europe, the UK[1]. The possible use of this by companies to protect themselves (ie. their managements) from takeover attempts is generally seen by investors as restricting free market behaviour and limiting full realisation of value for shareholders, and in this context the practice has been quite heavily criticised from many quarters. Counter arguments can be put forward in terms of, for example, long-term versus short-term targets and achievements for a company, but this debate is too complex to be described here.

During periods of particularly intense takeover activity, there will tend to be a greater speculative element in the share prices of companies with unrestricted shareholdings/voting rights. However, in other periods, there may be little to differentiate types of share and it may hardly seem worthwhile to pay anything extra for voting rights. This may be especially true for small scale investors: a small number of votes is unlikely to be seen as influential in company decision-making. Votes are more relevant for powerful institutional investors who may well voice opinions on company affairs, especially those relevant to share price and dividend performance. Dividend guarantees, as offered by preference shares, may be more useful, therefore, to some investors than voting rights. However, this is not simply the equivalent of holding a (low coupon) bond as preference shares still offer an opportunity of capital gains/losses alongside the ordinary share price.

---

[1]   For further details of other markets and share classes see ALLEN, M. :'The Times Guide to International Finance', Times Books 1991.

2. Pricing

How do investors assess the appropriate price or value of a 'membership right security', ie. a share? As indicated above, in stable conditions, the shares of large, mature companies may seem very similar to bonds, offering a regular dividend payment and repayment of capital on sale of the security. In these cases, the share price could be assessed using a discount formula equivalent to that applied in bond pricing and such a model is described in section 2.1 below.

However, a share may not be worthless even if it pays no dividend. It may be that dividends are expected in the future (as with small, high growth companies) or that the shareholder is 'rewarded' by a rising share price. It should not be forgotten that a share is an ownership right, thus the share price should rise alongside a company's net assets (such an asset valuation may be particularly pertinent for property companies, for example). In theory, an investor's preference for being 'paid' in dividends or share price gains should only be influenced by factors such as tax treatment or transactions costs.

Another method of assessing a share's value, or price, is by comparing the total expected return with a risk-free return (eg. money market rate) plus a risk premium, which is based on historical analysis of price behaviour and risk. This methodology comes from Arbitrage Pricing Theory. Another result linked to the Capital Asset Pricing Model is that only some risk is rewarded and therefore investors must be wary of equating risk taking with higher expected returns. These concepts are discussed in the following sections.

2.1 Dividend discount models

Dividend discount and present market value represent probably one of the oldest theory-related attempts to explain share prices. The basic idea is the same as for pricing bonds: the price of the asset – in principle, here, the value of the company – is made up of the present value (ie. weighted, or discounted, sum) of all future yields. For shares, these yields are determined by two (variable) elements:

- The (expected) stream of dividends
- The (expected) price development of the share

This highlights an important difference between the pricing of a share and the pricing of a bond. Whilst for bonds, it is possible to work with values fixed by contract (coupon and repayment), it is only possible in this case to work with expected values. This means that the flow of payments resulting from share ownership basically has to be estimated.

The value of a share according to the dividend discount model is therefore defined as the current value of all **expected** future dividends.

$$
(3.1) \qquad P_t = \frac{D_1}{(1+k)} + \frac{D_2}{(1+k)^2} + \ldots + \frac{D_n}{(1+k)^n} = \sum_{i=1}^{n} \frac{D_i}{(1+k)^i}
$$

where $P(t)$ =   share price at time t
           $D(i)$ =   expected dividend paid during period i
           k =   a 'suitable' discount (interest) rate

It is obvious that the equation (3.1) provides a simple cash valuation, as we found in bond analysis. But in using such models in equity analysis, several critical assumptions have to be made. Let us consider some of the problems which arise.

Point 1:

One plausible objection to the above model is the seemingly implied assumption that an investor buys the share during time t (using the above model) with the intention of never selling it again (the time factor, n, in a sense becomes infinite). However, in reality, a share may be bought and sold regularly because the investor realises short-term capital gains. On the other hand, it can be shown that even if we take into account that the share is only kept for a certain period of time, the pricing equation (3.1) is still valid.

In such a case, payments would consist of the expected dividend in Year 1 (D1) and the expected price at the end of the period (P1). The price at the start of the investment (P$_0$) would then be:

(i) $$ P_0 = \frac{D_1}{(1+k)} + \frac{P_1}{(1+k)} $$

At the end of Period 1 the share will then be sold on to someone who again has only a time span of one period. His price equation would then be:

(ii) $$ P_1 = \frac{D_2}{(1+k)} + \frac{P_2}{(1+k)} $$

If we now introduce (ii) into (i), this becomes

(iii)
$$P_0 = \frac{D_1}{(1+k)} + \frac{D_2}{(1+k)} + \frac{P_2}{(1+k)^2}$$

This can now be repeated over several time periods and the final result (n infinite) would again be

(iv)
$$P_0 = \frac{D_1}{(1+k)} + \frac{D_2}{(1+k)^2} + \ldots + \frac{D_n}{(1+k)^n} = \sum_{i=1}^{n} \frac{D_i}{(1+k)^i} \quad \text{q.e.d.}$$

Hence, the value of a share in this Dividend Discount Model is basically equal to the discounted value of all future dividend payments, ie. equal to (3.1).

Point 2:

The discount rate k has to be determined. This problem is similar to that in bond analysis and the solution we suggested there was to take an interest rate corresponding to the investment risk, thus allowing for some premium as opposed to a risk-free investment. In this case, the premium is usually considered to be higher than that for bonds as the risks for shares are, as a rule, higher than those for interest-guaranteed notes. However, it can also be assumed here that the discount rate, k, will fluctuate with the general interest rate level (ie. there is a constant, or at least reasonably stable, risk premium).

Point 3:

D(t), the yield or dividend payment, is an **expected** sum that cannot be fixed, even though it must be explicitly specified in the equation. Valuation will thus vary according to changes in the expected development of dividend payments, which may be a highly subjective assessment.

To sum up, equation (3.1) and the points made above imply that the value of a share fluctuates not only according to the development of the capital market yield (via k), as in the case of bonds (provided the debtor does not declare himself bankrupt), but also depends on **dividend expectations.** It follows that the equity market will, as a rule, be exposed to more severe (expectations-driven) fluctuations than the bond market, or, at least, the stockmarket will be influenced by a greater number of factors suggesting greater potential for creating variability in prices. The illustration below provides empirical evidence of this volatility differential for equity and bond markets.

Comparison of volatility
US equity and bond markets

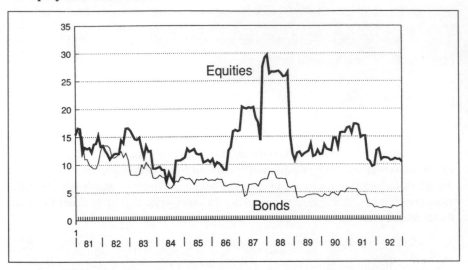

The chart shows that during the 1980s volatility in bonds (US bonds index) remained low and even decreased whilst in the equity market (S&P 500) volatility clearly increased dramatically. The chart also shows the impact the stockmarket Crash of autumn 1987 had on volatility for the subsequent period. We will return to the subject of the ways and means of estimating volatility later, indeed the table on page 41 is a good illustration of the volatility differential between bonds and equities for the major markets.

In general, a rather complex Dividend Discount Model, as in example (3.1), can be simplified by making certain assumptions as to how the amount of dividend paid will change during any given time period. The two most popular approaches are discussed briefly in the following section.

2.2 Constant dividends

It is possible to simplify valuations by, for example, assuming a constant annual dividend. In this case, a 'perpetuity' would be added into the price equation (an infinite number of payments of equal size). The price formula would thus be:

(3.2) $$P_0 = \frac{D}{(1 + k)} + \frac{D}{(1 + k)^2} + \ldots + \frac{D}{(1 + k)^\infty}$$

where D signifies the constant dividend in each period. The present value of such a perpetuity is defined as follows:

$$(3.3) \qquad P_0 = \frac{D}{k}$$

Equation (3.3) reminds us of the formula for the dividend yield, that is:

$$\text{Dividend yield} = \frac{D}{P_0}$$

This shows how much the direct yield of an equity investment would be, if a constant dividend were to be assumed. Combining this and (3.3), we can define the present value, P_0, as that value which equates the dividend yield with discount rate k. Just as the price of a bond has to change in response to general interest rates, to maintain the attractiveness of the investment, so too must a share price change in order to match the dividend yield with k (which fluctuates with market interest rates).

How realistic is a constant dividend? If it is assumed that company dividend payments should actually tend to increase over time, then a constant dividend payment suggests a retention of capital for reinvestment. However, such investments, as a rule, are expected to lead to higher future profits, and increasing company profits should ultimately lead to an increase in the dividends paid out, which contradicts the constant dividend assumption. This leads us to the following alternative model.

2.3 Constant dividend growth

As an alternative to the assumption of dividends remaining constant, it can more reasonably be assumed from the above discussion that dividend payments are likely to increase at a more or less constant rate. This assumption is used in the following model:

$$(3.4) \qquad D_t = D_0 (1 + g)^t$$

where g is assumed to be the (constant) dividend growth rate.

If this is substituted into equation (3.1), then after some reworking, we arrive at:

$$(3.5) \qquad P_0 = \frac{D_1}{(k - g)} \quad \text{and} \quad P_1 = P_0 (1+9)$$

The current share value is calculated from the next period's expected dividend, D_1, which is discounted in this model by the difference between the risk-adjusted capital market yield and the dividend growth rate (assumed to be constant). The share price will be expected to grow over time at the same rate, g, as the dividend and the higher g is, the higher the initial price, Po, becomes. The share price, Po, is the value which equates the total return expected with discount rate k. It is clear from the equation that this model would only give sensible results if $k > g$, ie. if the discount rate is higher than dividend growth. If g varies over time, however, it may be possible for some particular period for $g > k$. This problem, together with the relatively restrictive assumptions required by the model, has led to the development of more complex dividend discount models, and will undoubtedly lead to more still. Nevertheless, these complex models are so far no more popular than the more simplistic approaches and it would go beyond the framework of this introduction to go deeper into this subject[1], although the basic concept of the dividend discount appraisal should be understood.

It is important to note that there are essentially three determining factors of a share price, and its volatility, in all dividend discount models:

1. the capital market yield
2. the dividend and profit expectations for a company
3. its economic potential

Company-specific factors come into the equation only indirectly. In fact, dividend discount models are exclusively investment-specific and not company-specific pricing models. As such they may be more applicable to 'mature' companies with high payout ratios and stable dividend policies. Accordingly, dividend discount models may be said to follow rather than predict share price developments. For example, a new growth stock paying no dividends over several periods may appear practically worthless in such a model. As an alternative, therefore, 'earnings yield models' may be used. These are basically constructed along the lines of the dividend discount model and are similarly derived, however, they not only consider the distributed profit (the dividend), but also the profits (earnings) of the company as a whole. We might also reflect again on the similarity of bonds and equities as the more uncertainty is removed, the more the return on equities (dividend yield plus price gains) should be close to the return on an equivalent bond (an arbitrage condition). For a large mature company operating in a stable economic environment, we have already

---

[1] Compare this instance BRIGHAM, EF.: 'Financial Management', Theory & Practice, Chicago, New York: Dryden Press 1985, and references therein.

indicated that the dividend discount model assuming constant dividend growth may be deemed applicable. If the likelihood of takeovers or closing down is minimal, then such a company's share should exhibit little risk premium compared with a bond of infinite life and constantly growing coupon payment. In equilibrium, therefore, k (which equals the total expected return) should be close to the interest rate on long-term bonds, an arbitrage condition which in some way points us towards the Capital Asset Pricing Model and Arbitrage Pricing Theory described later in this chapter.

3. Fundamental analysis

Fundamental equity analysis focuses on company evaluation and the prediction of profit development. The methods applied are, in principle, the same as those used in bond rating or credit analysis in commercial banking. The process is based on both the classic methods of balance sheet and profit and loss analysis, and on the analysis of a number of key ratios which are seen as most relevant to an equity investor. It should not be forgotten that the ultimate aim of the analysis in this context is the assessment of the potential gains from investment via equity holdings. The analysis focuses on the most relevant points for an investor rather than being a totally comprehensive survey, and much emphasis is placed on judgmental forecasts.

The main difficulty in evaluating equity investments – as already noted above – lies in the assessment of the overall outlook for a company, with uncertainties being exacerbated by the fact that its profit and dividend potential will also be subject to the influence of changing economic conditions. A company analyst must therefore continuously reassess the outlook using data such as the balance sheet, profit and loss statements and press announcements, and the results must be subjected to further analysis in order to make some judgement regarding the current stockmarket valuation. Only in this way will it be possible to establish some systematic method-ology for identifying under or over-valued situations thus justifying buying or selling strategies for individual shares.

All companies quoted on a stock exchange are regularly subjected to such fundamental analysis by the financial research departments of the major banks and securities houses. As a rule, it is not enough to sift through annual reports and other 'secondary material'. Normally, analysts undertake much more detailed reviews, usually requiring 'management interviews', in which they try to establish in more detail the business strategies of the companies in question. These interviews are an important information and contact source for equity analysts, as the summary statistics (balance sheets, profit and loss statements etc.) available in annual reports often provide only a minimal basis for analysis with little qualitative appreciation of the company's strategy and outlook.

3.1 Balance sheet analysis

Balance sheet analysis relates to the examination of the structure of assets and liabilities in a company balance sheet. This type of analysis is perhaps most interesting when comparing a cross-section of different companies in the same sector or in a dynamic context. Otherwise, balance sheet analysis, as a single company snapshot, often contains relatively little investment information. Balance sheet ratios are typically calculated to reflect the main features of a balance sheet in a condensed form. Ratios give information on, for example, financing (capacity for self-financing investment from cashflow), asset structure, liquid funds, the indebtedness of a company and the structure of this debt. To illustrate this point, one commonly used ratio is the debt/equity ratio (ie. net borrowing/shareholders' funds).

It would be beyond the scope of this book to discuss the particular figures in more detail. The interested reader is directed towards the relevant specialist literature.[1] However, it will be clear how such information affects investment advice: high debt levels may call into question ability to service debt, threatening the survival of the company and reducing any possible compensation to shareholders in the event of bankruptcy. Substantial asset holdings (eg. cash, valuable surplus property, brand names) may offset debt and enhance the share price. Analysis of the debt structure may also aid appraisal of the quality of management of the firm (financing debt at best rates, obtaining returns on assets?) It should not be forgotten that shareholders own the company and, therefore, asset value (as well as earnings and dividend stream) is relevant to the valuation of a 'share'. For some companies (eg. property sector), the net asset value provides a measure of a share's theoretic price whereas other companies may generate profits with virtually no assets so that share pricing is based on income stream.

3.2 Analysis of profit and loss statements

Profit and loss analysis examines in some detail how a company arrives at a profit/loss and thus the potential for future growth and dividend distribution. Here, a distinction is made between analysis of costs (labour, raw materials etc.), involving research into what company funds are actually spent on, and analysis of income, which details how revenue is generated in a company (types of goods/services sold, pricing, profit from rents and financial investments etc.). It is clear that systematic

---

[1] See for example LEVINE, S.N. (Ed.): 'The Financial Analyst's Handbook', Part Three, Second edition Business One Irwin, 1988 and references therein. Also GASKING, T.: 'Perfect Financial Ratios', Century Business 1993, O'GILL, J.: 'Practical Financial Analysis', Kogan Page Business Action Guides 1992 and TRACY, J.A.: 'How to Read a Financial Report', John Wiley, provide easily accessible material.

analysis of costs and revenues is essential for a company's own internal purposes, ie. as a management tool. But it is just as clear that it is extraordinarily difficult for external financial analysts to gain access to all the necessary detailed data. In many cases, they must be satisfied with aggregated and summary data and final figures. Profitability and cashflow information are the most commonly available data. Typical ratios calculated include:

- Return on Equity (%) $= \dfrac{\text{net profit x 100}}{\text{equity}}$

- Return on Assets (%) $= \dfrac{(\text{net profit} + \text{interest on external funds}) \times 100}{\text{total assets}}$

- Net Profit Margin (%) $= \dfrac{\text{net profit x 100}}{\text{turnover}}$

- Cashflow Margin (%) $= \dfrac{\text{cashflow x 100}}{\text{turnover}}$

- Cashflow as % of Capital Spending (self-financing ratio) $= \dfrac{\text{cashflow x 100}}{\text{investment expenditure}}$

- Interest Cover $= \dfrac{\text{Pre-tax and interest payments profit}}{\text{Interest paid}}$

- Dividend Cover $= \dfrac{\text{net profit}}{\text{total dividends paid}}$

Other interesting variables are operating margins, inventory levels and working capital. As already indicated, it is really the comparison of these fundamental data across companies (cross-section), or over time (dynamic analysis), which is most important and which enables the analyst to make a sensible judgement on the efficiency of management and potential profitability or possible changes in profitability of a company. Potential profitability is extremely important for investment and future profit development and, through distributed profit, ie. future dividends, it is also crucial for the equity price itself.[1] Comparisons of data for companies operating in different sectors or countries need to be used with caution as business needs or treatment of certain factors (such as depreciation or 'exceptional' items) can

[1] For a detailed analysis of these issues see: Foster, G.: 'Financial statement analysis', Englewood Cliffs, N.Y.: Prentice Hall 1986 or, as a short summary: Renwick, F.B.: 'Analysis of Financial Statements: Conventional and Modern' in Levine, S.N.: 'The Financial Analyst's Handbook' op. cit. pages 389-437.

vary greatly. For companies operating in very similar circumstances, more emphasis may be placed on comparisons of managerial ability regarding use/cost of working capital, inventory and debt controls etc. It should be noted that calculation of statistics such as net profit may not be straightforward due to a lack of consensus on how to treat some items (the 'exceptional' items mentioned above) such as one off gains/losses (eg land sales, restructuring costs or compensation claims). It is generally felt more appropriate for share prices to reflect longer term trends rather than be influenced too much by such 'exceptional' items but sometimes confidence can be affected by these.

3.3 Common ratios for share evaluation

Besides ratios solely concerned with a company's balance sheet and profit and loss statements, fundamental equity analysis also utilises other ratios relating to the share price itself, with the obvious intention of aiding assessment of investment potential. A few of the more important ones are:

- P/E Ratio (or PER) $= \dfrac{\text{share price}}{\text{earnings per share (EPS)}}$

- Earnings yield (%) $= \dfrac{\text{EPS} \times 100}{\text{share price}}$

- Price/Cashflow Ratio $= \dfrac{\text{share price}}{\text{cashflow per share (CFPS)}}$

- Dividend Yield (%) $= \dfrac{\text{dividend per share}}{\text{share price}}$

It is not necessary here to list and explain all the possible types of valuation ratios and their application. We should also note that some ratios are more important for some types of companies than others. As a brief example, dividend yield comparisons may be heavily stressed for mature, stable profit companies (typically utilities) but not for small, high growth potential companies (for which sales/revenue and operating margins projections over several years may be more useful). From the previous discussion of the dividend discount model, it is also easy to see the reason why the dividend yield is often compared to a benchmark bond yield to assess how relatively 'cheap' equities are versus bonds (the comparison may take the form of the differential, the 'yield gap', or the ratio, the 'yield ratio'). The dividend is considered in this case the 'income' from the equity held just as the coupon is on the bond and if little change is expected in securities' prices (the financial market outlook is rather 'flat'), then investors may require more similar 'income' yields from bonds and equities. However, the 'earnings yield' (the inverse of the PER) may also be compared to the bond yield, giving another measure of the valuation of equities versus bonds based on overall profitability not just distributed profit (ie. dividends). As we have already indicated, both retained and distributed profits are important in evaluating equities, at least for the medium to long-term potential.

The interested reader should again refer to the specialist literature mentioned in the footnote. However, two of the above ratios will be discussed briefly because of their outstanding importance in most investors' evaluation of shares and, indeed, in most reporting of share price statistics[1].

Over the past years, the **P/E Ratio (PER)** has become one seemingly indispensible fundamental indicator for equity investment appraisal. The PER shows how many times the profit per share is covered by the price per share. It is usually argued that the lower the PER, the 'cheaper' the share: the investor is paying less to 'buy' profits. However, as with any goods, it is only common sense to ask whether something 'cheap' is worth buying. In fact, it is essential to investigate the fundamental determining factors of the PER, and not just look at its absolute or relative value. For example, a low and/or declining share price could occur for reasons which have no immediate, or indeed obvious, impact on earnings (profits) per share. These reasons could be related to managerial changes, dividend policy, debt problems, etc. In this case the PER could potentially fall far below the market or sector average. This, in itself, is not necessarily a signal to buy as the root problem may not have been resolved. In this case, the share price could sink even further, even if the PER already seems low. On the other hand, it is also possible that the PER 'recovers' again, not through a share price recovery but only because the profit per share falls – another consequence of economic, structural and/or management problems. These considerations also make it clear that all the determinants of the PER, including profits, must be assessed in using this statistic for investment decisions. Historic profits based on the most recently published company figures are often not very informative, although they provide a 'track record'. If this record is erratic, it will be of little use (like a 'random walk') but a consistently strong performance tends to enhance investor confidence and argues in favour of a relatively high PER being acceptable: the investor is buying 'quality' earnings. Nevertheless, estimated future profits (for the current and/or following years) are required to assess investment value, and they are naturally subject to some degrees of uncertainty for any company, however 'blue chip'.

---

[1] See, for example, the stockmarket pages of financial newspapers.

Furthermore, it is important to recognise that the PER concept in investment theory can be seen as a 'pay-back' approach ('how many annual profits are needed until the investment is repaid?'), which neglects interest rate effects. PER analysis without consideration of the prevailing interest rate regime is therefore misleading. A rule of thumb to learn is that when interest rates are high, then generally lower PERs seem more appropriate, whereas at times of low interest rates, high PERs do not necessarily indicate an overvalued market or shares. This can be linked to the investor's appraisal of alternative investments in bonds and cash (if interest rates are low, these alternatives may not appear so attractive) and also the expected beneficial effects of low interest rates on economic and company activity (this being more important for some companies than others).

It should be clearly understood that PER comparisons cannot sensibly be used as an isolated concept of equity analysis and investment appraisal, although it is not uncommon to find PERs used in this way.

The **Dividend Yield** is another measure of 'value', or 'return' and one that has become of more widespread interest since the stockmarket crash of 1987. The crash of 1990 reinforced this view. A collapse of share prices leads – by definition – to increased dividend yields. In addition, the relatively strong economic situation which prevailed through much of the 1980s, creating earnings growth for most companies, led to a situation in which dividend payments were generally increasing rapidly. Many companies actually aim to achieve dividend continuity (even if this means dipping into reserves in poor profit periods) and shareholders have also come to believe in such continuity either because of expectations (possibly inaccurate) of continued profit growth or because of expected company commitments to dividend payments. For a long-term oriented investor, this may suggest that buying shares (at least in 'dividend friendly' companies) could give approximately the same direct return in the form of a dividend yield as buying bonds, but at the same time the investor would have purchased the opportunity to participate in a potential bull market, ie. share price increase. This may seem too good to be true, and indeed the risks should not be overlooked: share prices can go down as well as up (an official 'health' warning in some countries) and the belief in dividend continuity can be disappointed at times. In the recent prolonged 1990/1992 economic recession, investors have perhaps been served a reminder that dividends can indeed fall. In some cases, dividends are still being reduced in 1993. There are also important differences in treatment of shareholders in the unfortunate case of a company going into liquidation (not, however, a common occurence amongst the 'blue chip' leading companies).

4. Technical analysis

Fundamental equity analysis, the basics of which have already been outlined above, provides a route by which an investor may hope to seek out 'undervalued' securities and companies. It assumes, therefore, that the underlying or 'true' value of a share can be determined, or approximated, in some way using company specific data and economic parameters. Whilst the actual estimation of the value may be subject to some uncertainty, it is assumed that such a concept at least exists, and is crucial for investment appraisal.

This assumption has been criticised in many different ways. The following quote accurately characterises one of the directions of this criticism: "The stock market reflects not only the different valuation concepts of those who evaluate shares in an orthodox way (ie. fundamental analysts, the authors). It reflects just as much the hopes and fears, assumptions, feelings and voices – rational and irrational – of hundreds of potential buyers and sellers".[1]

There is no doubt, that in traditional fundamental analysis the psychological dimension of pricing in financial markets – we are not referring here to the stockmarkets alone, but to all markets – has for a long time been treated as a 'poor relation', and is still being treated this way in many places.

'Technical Analysis' has been derived in part as an answer to criticisms of the fundamental analysts' supposed neglect of market phenomena and it has, at least implicitly, attempted to satisfy several psychological factors. The technical analyst generally operates on the hypothesis that prices in financial markets form a certain pattern over time which tends to be repeated in a similar way and is therefore of use in a valuation analysis. Such analysts believe that knowledge of technical methods is becoming more important for success in investment. Some believe that the reason for this may be due to something like a self-fulfilling prophecy if enough investors actively use such techniques. Hopes of spiralling success are wrong, of course, because as soon as a certain technique influences a price in a systematic way, making price movements predictable, enough investors/traders will be on hand to use this same information, thus necessarily destroying the success of the discovered technique. That is, once a technique becomes utilised and familiar, the users are in a sense 'picked-off' by other traders who quickly learn the system and how to manipulate it – and thus it self-destructs.

---

[1] EDWARDS, R.D./MAGEE, J.: 'Technische Analyse von Aktientrends', Darmstadt 1976, page 77, translation by the authors.

Technical analysis has found many forms of expression.[1] The form used most often is 'Chart Analysis', the working instrument being exclusively price charts usually with various moving averages superimposed. Other widely used techniques are the concepts of 'relative strength', 'filter rules', 'point and figure analysis', amongst others. It is impossible here to go into more detail about the many different techniques. If interested, the reader should look at the literature mentioned in the footnotes. However, all methods of technical analysis have one feature in common: they only use past price developments as a basis for price predictions.

The frequent use of excessively simplified analogies and the complete absence of theoretical logic for presumed price developments have lead to a situation in which technical analysis is generally not taken seriously in academic circles. But the situation is actually rather similar to that of time series analysis in economics, the usual consensus being that this is typically most useful in very short-term analysis and forecasting (eg. assessing momentum) and when behaviour cycles are very regular[2]. It is usually assumed that explanation, and prediction, of irregularities is best treated by fundamental analysis.

More recent theoretical developments indicate that certain forms of technical analysis can provide a little more than is usually expected of them, and they may also be able to treat irregularities which could be caused by discontinuities in relationships, ie. rather small changes in fundamental variables may suddenly cause massive fluctuations in markets whereas previously only small changes had been observed due to the mathematical characteristics of the functions linking these variables. It should be realised that mathematical concepts such as 'catastrophe theory' or 'chaos theory', suggest the possibility of price patterns existing which could be verifiable by technical methods (the difficulty with such complex mathematical concepts is usually at the stage of estimation and verification, which is necessary to fulfil the practical requirements for forecasting). Preliminary studies in this area have already been published and it would not be surprising if new forms of technical analysis were to be created from this. However, in order for these to be taken seriously, they must also be able to provide for falsifiable hypotheses. In this respect, they should not be the same as today's technical methods (of which there seem to be nearly as many as there are technical analysts).

---

[1] For a systematic explanation of the existing methods, PRING, M.J.: 'Technical Analysis Explained', New York: McGraw-Hill, Third edition. SHAW, A.R.: 'Market Timing and Technical Analysis', in : LEVINE, S.N.: 'The Financial Analyst's Handbook' op. cit. pages 312-372.
[2] See, for example, BERNSTEIN, J.: 'Cycles of Profit', Harper Collins; MILLARD, B.J.: 'Channel Analysis', John Wiley; PLUMMER, T.: 'Forecasting Financial Markets', Kogan Page.

In order to highlight the problems many investors have with chart analysis, the following brief (technical) analysis of the Japanese stockmarket is quoted. It appeared in a Swiss financial newspaper (translation by the authors):

"If there are more people already owning certain shares, than people who actually want them, take advantage of strength to sell ..... In this situation, not only do 'Top' formations in the price charts emerge, but the auxiliary indicators no longer confirm price advances. Out of 220 analysed shares, 161 (ie. an overwhelming 73%) show 'Top' characteristics, and only 59 (27%) show characteristics of trend continuation. Most of these 161 shares will come back and test support levels. If these tests fail, and the probability of this is high, supply will grow and demand will be discouraged. A continuation of what has already been started is then unavoidable: the trend is then one of falling prices. The most convincing argument for the theory that a Bear Market has started in Tokyo is the fact that the 'Top' patterns have appeared amongst the leading favourites at home and abroad."

"As always, the question of what has to happen in order to cause a change in opinion arises. Relatively a lot in Tokyo. One way this could arise is if the 'Tops' in the majority of the problematic individual shares were to be surpassed, which in the Tokyo Stock Exchange would seem to require surpassing the current market high with the upward move being confirmed by auxiliary indicators (volume, momentum, relative strength and breadth of the market). The alternative may be a longer sideways movement, which would demonstrate the capability of the market to absorb selling pressure which could create the basis for encouraging new demand."

In this case, it is not a question of whether or not the prediction of falling Japanese share prices is, or was, right or wrong. The problem which arises concerns the assumptions of such technicians. The text appears to contain such a large number of hypotheses that it is hardly possible to check what the relevant assumptions really are. This rather critical attitude towards technicians should not be taken too negatively – to be fair, the above quote has been taken out of context. It is quite possible that technical analysis could develop fruitfully, for example through investigating the possibilities for applying complex mathematical concepts. It might thus be seen as more of a mathematical complement to fundamental analysis than a competitor.

5. Risk concepts

So far in this chapter we have proceeded in a similar fashion to the section on bonds. First of all a number of definitions and institutional questions concerning equities had to be clarified, and then price setting, or valuation of shares, had to be explained. At this stage, it is also necessary to tackle the concept of risk. However, the analysis and measurement of risk takes on a somewhat different status in equity analysis than in bond analysis, because a number of theoretical questions arise in the discussion of equity risk which have become almost as important as equity analysis itself. Occasionally this goes so far that the concepts of equity analysis discussed in the previous section, by which investors searched for 'inner values', over and under-valuation, and the like, become known as **traditional** equity or financial analysis. In contrast, more recent approaches to investment appraisal dealing explicitly with specific risk concepts, share price correlations and relationships etc. are awarded the term '**modern** equity analysis'. As in most generalisations, these are also muddled and there is no doubt that both concepts of analysis play an important part within truly modern financial analysis. We will return to this point.

In the preceeding sections, individual equities and securities were treated in a rather isolated way and justifiably so given the interesting question of how much price potential a share has to have in order to indicate that a company is 'cheap'. Possible connections between price developments of different companies' shares were of no interest in this context. However, if we are concerned with broader investment decisions, in this sense more along the lines of portfolio management, analytical methods do exist to address and make use of these interactions. Here, the analyst no longer seeks exclusively to predict price potential or to judge the market value of a company, he must also make predictions about volatility and correlations ie. assess risks of both individual investments and **investment combinations** in the broadest sense.

In the following sections we will become acquainted with various risk concepts before discussing investment combinations within the framework of modern portfolio theory in a later chapter.

5.1 Variance and standard deviation

An intuitively plausible risk concept is volatility, ie. the **range** of fluctuations of a financial asset's return around its respective mean. It is clear that in the two graphs below, financial asset A is more 'risky' than financial asset B, although both yield exactly the same average profit or return (R) to the investor. Short term buy/sell, ie. trading, strategies offer a greater opportunity for gain (or loss) with A than B, however.

Asset A   **Asset B**

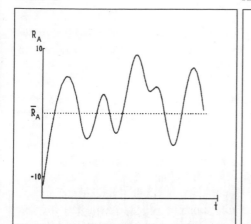   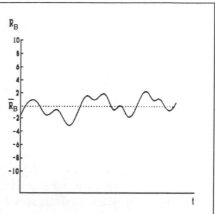

The vertical axes of the above graphs represent returns (price changes as a percentage against the previous period), and the horizontal axes represent a certain time period. Whilst financial asset B yields a profit between -2% (at the worst) and +3% (at the best points) over time, there is the chance with financial asset A of reaching +10% at one time but losing the same (-10%) at another time. Ranges of variation, as shown above, are known as 'volatility' or 'risk'. With the help of the statistical concept of 'variance', it is possible to find a unit of measurement for this risk, as defined below:

$$(3.6) \qquad \text{Variance} = \frac{1}{n} \sum_{t=1}^{n} (R_t - R_m)^2$$

This is the average (n is the figure to watch) of the square of the fluctuations in the respective return R_t from its mean value R_m.[1] The larger the unit of measurement of R, the bigger the fluctuations, and according to the variance, the bigger the apparent risk undertaken by an investor, ie. the variance is dependent on the units of measurement used. For this reason, in practice, the 'risk' concept relates not to the variance, or sum of the squared fluctuations, itself, but its square root, the so-called 'standard deviation'.

---

[1] Sometimes variance definitions are given indicating division by n-1. This is because when calculating the mean value (R_m), one degree of freedom is in principle lost. This difference, however, is only of marginal importance for large values of n, and need not concern the layman.

(3.7)   Standard deviation = $\sqrt{\text{variance}}$

The following charts show the monthly price changes of US equities (S&P 500) over the last decade, as well as the corresponding price changes of US bonds over the same period.

US share index: % monthly price changes

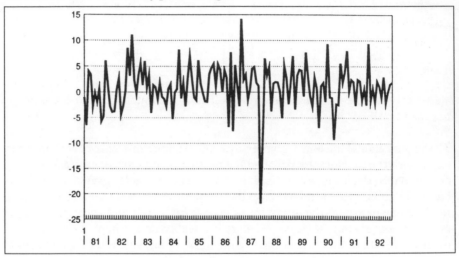

Bond index (US average): % monthly price changes

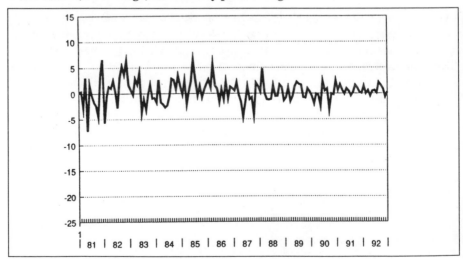

We have already met a counterparty to the above graphs at the beginning of this Chapter. Section 2.1 showed how strongly bond risks differed from equity risks. These two graphs also illustrate this quite impressively. The average annual standard deviations are 14% for the equity price changes and 8% for the bond price changes.

As a rule, the standard deviation calculated from historical data is used as an indicator of how risky a certain investment is likely to be in the future, or how strongly returns will fluctuate around a certain mean, ie. expected value. If an investor is prepared to make certain assumptions about the distribution of these returns[1], then it is possible to deduce from statistical theory that in two out of three cases the returns actually (ex-post) realised can be expected to fall within one standard deviation above or below the expected value. Furthermore, it can be expected that in nineteen out of twenty cases (95%) the realisation will fall within two standard deviations above or below the mean expected return. This is illustrated in the diagram on the next page.

This might sound academic. However, as a concrete example, this means that given a standard deviation of 20% per annum – a rather realistic size for a stockmarket – and an expected return (price change) of 8% over the next twelve months, then after one year there is a 33.3% probability that the actual return will be outside the +28% to -12% region (expected return +/- one standard deviation), and a probability of 5% of being outside the +48% to -32% range (expected return +/- two standard deviations). This shows the realistic risks of investing in any stockmarket. It is important to understand that this concept is symmetrical. Thus, risk is not understood to be pure risk of loss, but also as a chance of profit.[2]

The following table contains a calculation of standard deviations for most of the world's important bond and stockmarkets (calculated as average annualised standard deviations of monthly price changes over the periods 1980 to 1991). Clearly the risks in individual markets are not all the same.

---

[1] A normal (bell-shaped, symmetric) distribution (see chart on next page) is assumed here; an assumption which seems not too far away from reality.
[2] We remember here the assumption of the symmetric, bell-shaped normal distribution for the potential returns. A non-symmetric distribution could exist instead and this might create a different risk of loss than gain. However, there would still be a positive chance of higher returns.

Volatility of the major bond and stockmarkets		(Annualised average) 1980–1991	
		bonds	equities
USA	(S & P 500)	8	14
Japan	(Tokyo Dow Jones)	6*	16
Italy	(BCI)	2*	23
France	(CAC general)	6*	20
Germany	(FAZ)	5	16
UK	(FTSE 100)	8	17
Switzerland	(SBC general)	3	13

1985-1991 inclusive

Standard deviations, or volatility measures, have become more widely tracked with the creation of options markets. Volatility is an important determining factor of options premiums. If the usual option pricing models are used to calculate volatility with the premiums given (treated as an exogenous factor), then this becomes an estimate of future volatility, so-called 'implicit volatility', which can be seen as an alternative measure to historic standard deviation. This calculation provides more of a guide to expected volatility, as revealed in options market behaviour, rather than the backward-looking statistic of standard deviation represented by the past behaviour of the market. The options market actually incorporates any new information on the likely pattern of share price fluctuations (eg. changes in shareholder base, regulatory effects).

A normal distribution centred around the mean expected future share price

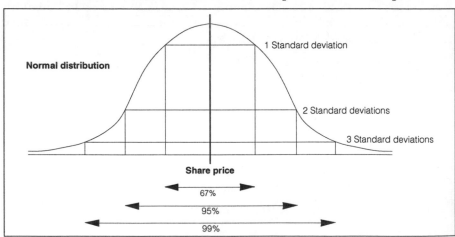

Probability distributions for high and low volatility stocks

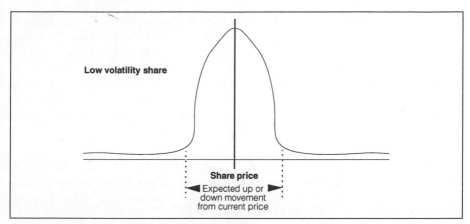

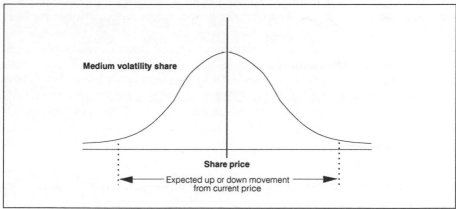

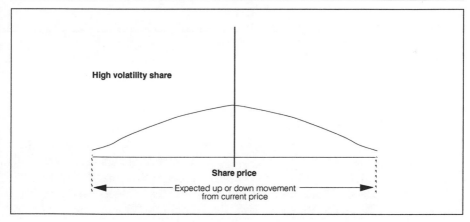

5.2 The index model

Variances and standard deviations are statistical measures of the scale of fluctuations in returns from investment in individual shares or the stockmarket. However, experience with stockmarkets tells us that fluctuations in individual share prices rarely take place in isolation. On the contrary, most fluctuations somehow occur simultaneously. In other words, for much of the time, share prices tend to go up or down with the market. These observations are put to good use in the 'index model', often called the 'market model', and this concept makes it possible to differentiate between alternative risk concepts and risk management.

The philosophy of the market, or index, model is based on the view that certain factors create general price movements in the stockmarket, and it therefore makes sense to interpret the price development of individual shares in the light of general market trends and the development of a share index.

The following graph attempts to illustrate this relationship. IBM has been chosen as the individual security, and the S&P 500 index represents the market.

Share returns and index returns – 1980-1991
(Example IBM)

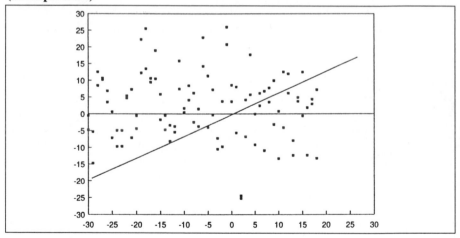

The vertical axis shows the average quarterly price changes of the IBM share price from 1980 to 1991, and the horizontal axis shows the quarterly changes of the S&P 500 index over the same period. The graph clearly shows that high index returns go together with high share returns, and vice versa. It is also clear that the relationship is fairly linear. These observations are not only valid for IBM shares, but they are more or less a general phenomenon. Even if all the graphs for individual shares are not exactly the same as the one above, they all have a broadly similar characteristic pattern. It is hard to find a truly contrarian share price! In theory, therefore, the index model can be described by the following formula:

(3.8) $R_{it} = \alpha_i + \beta_i \cdot R_{mt} + \varepsilon_{it}$

in which R_{it} represents the return (% price change) of the share i in period t, R_{mt} stands for the price change in the market portfolio (or index) in period t, α_i and β_i are constant company-specific parameters (we will come back to these later) and ε_{it} is an error term, taking into account the fact that such a simplified equation as (3.8) cannot, in reality, be truly accurate all the time. The straight line drawn in the above graph represents equation (3.8) for the IBM share. The ε in the equation therefore represents the actual deviations from the calculated estimates as represented by the straight line.[1]

Let us assume that the term ε is on average zero. The consequence of this is that the term $\beta_i R_{mt}$ represents that part of the share price change which is 'explained' by movements in the market, and α_i measures 'company specific' changes in the share price.

There is no real pricing theory behind the market model. It is purely a statistical description or breakdown of the relationship between the rate of change of a share price and an index. Furthermore, it is possible to estimate parameters α and β for all shares with a particularly simple statistical method.

If we take such an estimation for the above IBM example, it looks like this:

R (IBM)$_t$ = -1.6 + 0.9 R (Index)$_t$

In connection with the above graph, this equation can be interpreted as follows: α_i (-1.6) represents the point of intersection of the straight line and the vertical axis at point zero, indicating the size of return the IBM share is expected to provide even if the index remains completely unchanged within a certain period. Parameter β (0.9) is the slope coefficient of the straight line, measuring the sensitivity of the IBM share to changes in the index. A value for β greater than 1 implies that the share is fluctuating more strongly than the market, ie. fluctuating strongly upwards or downwards. A value smaller than 1 implies that the share reacts less than the index. It therefore becomes clear that β is, in effect, a measurement of volatility or risk. The smaller the β-value is estimated to be for a single share, the less the return on the share fluctuates alongside changes in the index, and, conversely, the larger the value, the more the return on the share fluctuates.

---

[1]   In fact, the straight line is estimated (eg. using estimation procedures as simple as ordinary least squares) from the cluster of data points available and the term ε represents the usual 'white noise term' with an expected value of zero.

Consequently, the market model shows that the fluctuations of a share price are based on two different classes of influential variable:

(i)   factors influencing the market as a whole, such as the economic and political environment, market psychology, etc. These factors are reflected in the term $\beta_i R_{mt}$.

(ii) company specific factors, such as new discoveries, technology or management, and any events particularly influencing α_i and ε_{it}.

That part of the risk which is caused by market specific factors is usually described as 'systematic risk' in the literature, while the remainder of volatility is called 'non-systematic' or 'equity-specific risk'. Parameter β above is therefore the indicator for the systematic risk of a share.

β plays a very important part in modern portfolio theory. It is usually assumed that taking greater risks leads to higher expected returns. But in this context it is clear that such an assumption is only true in the case of systematic risk, because non-systematic, ie. company specific risk, can be diversified away by the careful structuring of a portfolio. We will come back to this point in more detail in the section on Modern Portfolio Theory.

It has already been pointed out that a market model can basically be estimated for any share. Therefore, the accuracy of the estimated model (ie. how 'close' the points are to the straight line) must be variable, ie. the market model accounts for different proportions of the volatility in share prices. There is a statistic which can be used to measure the proportion of the variation in the return on a share accounted for by the market model. This statistic, R^2, indicates the explanatory power of the market model. R^2 lies between 0 and 1, eg. as an example it may be 0.6. This means that 60% of the total variation of this share's return can be 'accounted for' by variations in the index.

The following table gives, as an example, estimates for α_i, β_i and R^2 for some of the major Swiss shares. It is clear that these values vary considerably, which is a very important source of information for the investor.

	α_i	β_i	R^2
Alusuisse	0.71	0.95	0.29
Bâloise	1.95	1.00	0.37
BBC	1.72	0.90	0.39
Elektrowatt	-0.28	0.87	0.69
Feldschlösschen	0.01	0.79	0.34
Globus	0.61	0.73	0.40
Holderbank	0.47	0.70	0.37
Nestlé	1.01	0.86	0.44
Sandoz	0.37	1.18	0.62
Schindler	0.20	1.39	0.51
CS Holding	-0.31	0.99	0.81
Swiss Re	0.98	0.80	0.58
Winterthur	0.56	0.84	0.49
Zürcher Ziegeleien	0.51	0.62	0.35
Zürich Ins	0.21	1.12	0.60

5.3 The index model in portfolio analysis

If we begin with the rather realistic assumption that equity-specific risks, as expressed by the ε terms in the above equation, are mainly independent, then these risks will tend to 'balance out' if we put together a portfolio of several equities. In principal, it is possible to 'diversify away' all equity-specific risks by holding sufficiently diversified portfolios. The more diversified the portfolios, the nearer to unity (100% explanatory power) the R^2 statistic should be, and the more the general market development would equate with the portfolio yield. In a portfolio composed to correspond to the index (in such a case, we are talking about a completely passive investment strategy in the stockmarket), the R^2 would, of course, be 1, α would be zero and the portfolio risk (by definition) would be a pure market risk ($\beta = 1$).

In the following table, we have put together various portfolios from the different shares for which α_i, β_i and R^2 estimates were shown in the previous table, and the portfolio properties have been calculated.[1]

Number of shares	α_p	β_p	R^2_p
3	1.5	0.95	0.59
7	0.6	0.93	0.85
15	0.4	0.95	0.90
20	0.3	0.96	0.92

As expected, as the number of shares in the portfolio increases, the values of α and β (systematic risk) tend towards zero and 1 respectively and R^2 also approaches unity. This corresponds with the statement that non-systematic (ie. company specific) risk tends towards zero.[2]

6. Capital asset pricing model (CAPM)

It has already been indicated above that the market, or index, model has no fundamental theory underlying it, and that it is simply a statistical description of the relationship between the return on a share and the return on the 'market'. However, it provides us with a new understanding of risk by explicitly pointing out that it is just as important whether share price fluctuations are based on fluctuations of the market as a whole or whether company specific events are making a share more or less attractive. The Capital Asset Pricing Model (CAPM) takes these considerations and problems and combines them with the results derived from Modern Portfolio Theory, basically that all non-systematic (company specific) risks can be diversified away, to form an equilibrium theory for financial markets.

The seemingly obvious statement that an investor should be 'rewarded' with a higher expected return for taking greater risks – why else should he take higher risks? – is the basis for this model. For the stockmarket, this means that an investor should be able to expect a higher return from a more risky share than from a less risky share, however we define 'risky'. This must be true to support the fact that somehow or other (in equilibrium) investors must be prepared to hold all the shares in the market. We will

---

[1] The results in this table are, naturally, somewhat arbitrary, as the portfolios were put together at random. To be more accurate, all possible portfolios should be calculated from the 20 shares, and then averages should have been taken. This was not done here, but it is not crucial to the argument.

[2] A lot of empirical work on these issues is presented in: WAGNER, W.A./LAU,S.: 'The Effect of Diversification on Risk', in: Financial Analyst Journal, 26, 1971, pages 48–53.

come back to this argument of equilibrium. In the CAP model, the previous discussion of systematic versus non-systematic risk is used to show that in 'pricing' assets it is not necessary to consider the entire risk of a security, but only systematic risk β. Taking non-systematic risks should **not** be rewarded by higher expected returns because such risks can basically be avoided. Loosely translated, this means that in a fully diversified portfolio, a higher return can be gained on average by taking a higher systematic risk, but not from an additional non-systematic risk stemming from insufficient diversification.

The suggestion that risk and (expected) return are positively correlated with each other is, of course, not new. This concept was also used when discussing bond prices (rating considerations in section 4.3, chapter II). This philosophy has been used for a long time in credit decisions, amongst other things, although the definition of risk may be different. Here, we have introduced the notion that it is not the entire risk of an investment which is relevant for its pricing, but only that part which cannot be avoided (ie. diversified away). The logic behind this method implies that investors cannot assume that they will be compensated by a correspondingly high expected return when taking above average company specific risks.

This concept can be illustrated by the following graph:

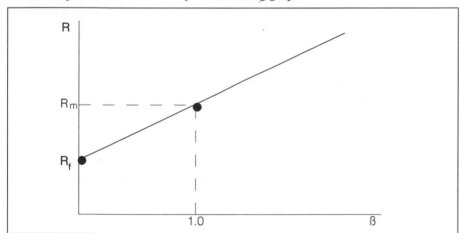

The graph resembles the one used for illustrating the market model. However, the standard deviation (volatility) is no longer represented on the horizontal axis, but systematic risk β instead. The straight line – known as the 'capital market line' – shows the (linear) relationship between expected return and (systematic) risk. A systematic risk of β = 1 (market risk) results in the market return (R_m). The starting point of the line is a risk-free interest rate R_f, which could, for example, correspond with a savings account interest rate with β = 0, ie expected returns not at all 'fluctuating with the market'. Naturally the risk increases as an investor moves along the line (β increasing), so some compensation in the form of a higher expected return is demanded for accepting this risk increase (the line is upward sloping). This compensation is the 'market price' of the risk, as defined by the difference between the risk-free return and the expected return (R_i - R_f).

From the above, we can see that the following equation can be formed for the expected yield of any one asset (i):

(9) $R_i = R_f + \beta_i (R_m - R_f)$

Furthermore, a term for the risk premium (expected yield differential) for any one asset can be formulated as follows:

(10) $(R_i - R_f) = \beta_i (R_m - R_f)$

Why is the Capital Asset Pricing Model called the equilibrium model of capital markets? The logic behind this is relatively simple and can be explained by the following graph:

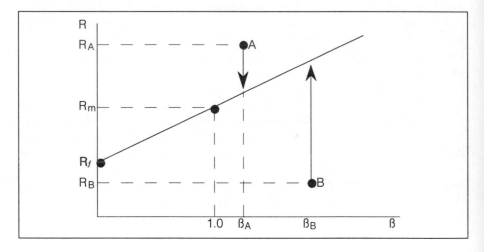

If, at any given time, there exists a financial asset A with the combination of (expected) return R_A and risk β_A as shown in the above graph, then this would immediately be recognised as undervalued. There would be an excess demand for asset A and the price of A would increase until (in equilibrium) the expected return fell back to the capital market line. The process would work in exactly the opposite direction in the case of an 'over-valued' asset such as B.

In this sense, the above straight line – the capital market line – is understood to be an 'equilibrium concept', enabling statements to be made as to whether a financial asset is over or under-valued at any given time, and how prices should react to eliminate such anomalies[1].

7. Arbitrage pricing theory (APT)

Already in this chapter we have shown that an asset's expected return can be said to be equal to a risk-free interest rate plus a risk premium commensurate with a measure of the risk of the asset. As we discovered in the CAP model discussion, this premium, or risk 'reward', can only cover systematic risk as non-systematic risk can be avoided (by diversification). The index model method of building portfolios was introduced as a way of eliminating non-systematic risk and a portfolio's systematic risk was defined relative to the market via beta, which provided a measure of the 'reward' of higher expected returns for risk taken.

However, there are a number of problems which arise with this method which have lead to the development of an alternative measurement of risk using APT. One problem is a practical difficulty of a choice of 'index'. The theoretical index portfolio should literally represent all possible investment opportunities but in practice 'index' funds usually adopt some quite narrow particular representation of the market as a benchmark, eg. the S&P 500 in the US, FTSE 100 in the UK, the CAC 40 in France, the DAX 30 in Germany. These indices actually represent only a selection of the largest (by market capitalisation) companies in each market, which does not guarantee an efficient portfolio. The reference portfolio constructed may not replicate 'the market' and the beta calculated will depend on the selection process. The main point for investors is that it becomes possible to find alternative portfolios (not discriminating in terms of size) which should, according to the principles of diversification, offer higher expected returns for the same risk (or lower risk for the same return) than the 'index' funds described. Fund managers have exploited this weakness in the 'index' model to offer portfolio management aimed at modestly outperforming a benchmark index (eg. S&P 500 in the US) without taking higher risk.

---

[1] For a more thorough summary of the single index and the CAPM-literature and the respective empirical work, see MODIGLIANI F./POGUE, G.A.: 'Risk, Return and CAPM: Concepts and Evidence' in: LEVINE, S.N.: 'The Financial Analyst's Handbook', op. cit. page 1139; also HAUGEN, R.A.: 'Modern Investment Theory', Woodhead Faulkner.

Attempts to outperform an index in this way can be based on stock-picking methods – searching for undervalued stocks for which the risk premium is judged somehow to be too high (using pricing analysis methods as described in this chapter in sections 2, 3 and 4). However, a more consistent approach is to make use of the alternative method of defining and measuring systematic risk which examines the actual underlying sources of risk and the premia which should be associated with the different factors (ie. how they should be 'rewarded'). APT has provided the basis for the development of this methodology of breaking down systematic risk into its component parts.

Generally, the sources of systematic risk are identified as unexpected changes in the fundamental economic factors, chiefly interest rates, inflation, business cycles and confidence. It is possible to show that portfolios which match a benchmark index, such as the DAX 30, may actually be very exposed to certain fundamental shocks such as business cycles (eg. if most of the large companies were to be 'cyclicals', ie. industrial concerns like chemicals). In terms of the APT method of measuring systematic risk, such 'index' portfolios should be considered as poorly diversified. Having identified/ measured the risks and premia, the risk exposures of the benchmark portfolio can be assessed and more efficient portfolios constructed by reweighting the exposure to certain types of risk (ie. those with more favourable risk/return ratios).

Clearly, one of the difficulties which arises with this method of managing portfolios is the identification and assessment of the risk factors, requiring use of a considerable amount of data and technical expertise in quantitative methods. One technique commonly used is factor analysis. These issues will not be treated further in this book, however.

Estimation processes are never entirely satisfactory and complex techniques will not be costless. Therefore, we would suggest that, in spite of their drawbacks, the simpler 'index' tracking systems may still have a place in fund management. The advantages and disadvantages of the products should at least be more familiar to investors.

The points made in the last few pages were of a rather theoretical nature and to some may not seem relevant in practice. In this case, it is simply worth noting that there is some outstanding evidence to prove that taking a substantial company specific risk will not, as a rule, be 'rewarded' and in this sense, careful portfolio diversification always pays. We will be occupied with this same question later, when we ask whether 'smaller' investors can really afford such diversification, or whether, given that smaller investors may not be able to diversify, they are actually being forced to take relatively greater risks than larger investors (institutional investors such as pension funds, insurance companies, etc.). This may seem ironic given that, as a rule, large institutions are perceived as better able to 'afford' such risks.

Chapter 4

Exchange Rate Theory

1. Introduction

It might seem surprising at first glance – especially if one refers back to the American tradition of financial market literature – to find a chapter on exchange rate theories in an introductory book on financial markets. The reason is because, on the one hand, the exchange rate is an important determinant of return in international portfolios – often equally important as the return on the equities and bonds contained in the portfolio – and, on the other, because 'price' determination on the foreign exchange markets is subject to similar basic principles as price determination on the equity and bond markets. In Anglo-American literature, in particular, this subject continues to be treated rather perfunctorily, most probably because the share of foreign assets in US portfolios is still relatively small.

On the subject of price determination on the foreign exchange markets and to exaggerate somewhat, we could say that if a share price reflects an assessment of the future prosperity of a company, the exchange rate represents something similar in the context of an assessment of a whole economy. For this reason, in the following sections, we will first briefly discuss the history of flexible exchange rates, then go on to price determination and finally derive certain implications for the behaviour of an international investor.

2. Fixed versus flexible exchange rates – the change in regime and its consequences

In contrast to what most people assume, flexible exchange rates – together with all the inherent problems they brought with them – were not first discovered in the 1970s. In the international history of money, there have indeed been periods in earlier centuries where experiments with flexible or quasi flexible exchange relationships between currencies were carried out. In the 1950s and 1960s, flexible exchange rates again became a popular policy recommendation, not least, given the growing inclination in academic circles, from a purely theoretic viewpoint, towards 'free market economics'. In this sense, the transition to flexible exchange rates in the early 1970s was in principle a kind of 'choice in favour of market forces' as a standard-setting instrument for the achievement of economic equilibria. In general, the opinion prevailing at the time was that a system of flexible exchange rates, after a probably turbulent transition phase, would find a stable balance relatively quickly: exchange rates would settle down to the so-called purchasing power parity level. This purchasing power parity level for exchange rates would be the level where a representative basket of goods in, for example, the USA would cost the same amount in dollars as it would in Germany. In all cases where this theory did not hold – ie. in the case where, for instance with a DM/US$ exchange rate of 2.00, the basket of goods cost $ 100 in New York and DM 150 in Frankfurt (ie. $ 75) – then goods would be exported from Germany to New York and vice versa. Keeping the argumentation very simple of course, this would lead to an increased supply of dollars on the foreign exchange markets (the importers have to pay for the German goods in DM) and in a free market environment this would lead in turn to a devaluation of the dollar, until such time as the two baskets of goods cost the same amount in both countries. This means the dollar would have devalued from DM/US$ 2.00 to 1.50.

Within this equilibrium model, the assumption was also made that speculation on the foreign exchange markets would have more of a stabilising than destabilising effect. Since speculators themselves would quickly recognise whether a currency was fundamentally (ie. in terms of purchasing power parity) over- or undervalued, this would ensure that large deviations from this equilibrium could not arise.

Although these theoretical reflections on the functioning of a free price formation system for currencies seem plausible enough, they are only relevant in practice to a very limited extent. Most importantly not even 10% of the volumes traded today on the foreign exchange markets are based on real goods flows – thus the goods arbitrage conditions with their corresponding foreign exchange volumes are practically irrelevant. Furthermore, if they wanted to stabilise the exchange rate at any specific equilibrium level, speculators would have to agree in some way on what this equilibrium level should be. However, neither purchasing power parity nor any other exchange rate equilibria can be determined objectively and/or each calculation of an equilibrium is of necessity based on a series of more or less arbitrary assumptions. This would in the end lead to there being a similarly large number of potential equilibria as there were speculators, which would of course render ineffective any attempted stabilising function of speculation.

With the benefit of hindsight, it is of course relatively easy to be critical of the optimism which characterised the transition to flexible exchange rates in the 1970s. But at the time, floating was indeed widely viewed as a reasonable alternative to a system of fixed rates, which had undoubtedly become unacceptable and unworkable for a variety of reasons.

The decisive question seems to be for which parameters of the economic system is volatility more (or less) tolerated by market participants. A conflict of interests exists, for example, on the question of whether volatility in monetary policy variables such as the interest rate or money supply, will create more or less problems than allowing volatility in the exchange rate. In an ideal world, most probably we would all choose to have both stable interest rates and money supply development and also stable exchange rates (unless we are speculators perhaps?). Since, however, these preferences are most likely to prove unrealistic, in practice we are typically faced with the problem of deciding in which area of the economy the volatility of economic variables 'does the least harm'. Fluctuations in the exchange rate are at least transparent and if one subscribes to the view that the system cannot eliminate volatility as such, then it would appear reasonable to 'leave' it where it is most transparent rather than forcing it into an area of the economy where it may be less obvious but not less damaging.

The early 1970s did indeed represent a milestone in recent history of exchange rates. They marked the collapse of the so-called BRETTON WOODS era of fixed rates and the transition to floating rates.

The BRETTON WOODS system of fixed exchange rates was inaugurated at the international conference held at Bretton Woods in New Hampshire in 1944. This followed a phase characterised by so-called 'competitive devaluations'. Through devaluation a country can make its goods artificially cheaper abroad and can thus, at the 'cost' of other countries, become more 'competitive' – ie. stimulate its export sector.

Thus, like every change to the system in the field of international monetary policy, BRETTON WOODS was designed to bring more stability. Its set goals were similar in a way to the earlier principles of the gold standard, under which the major currencies were fixed against gold and thus also amongst themselves.[1] The aim was to create an international monetary order in which exchange rates were fixed but not immovable, and to achieve as complete as possible convertibility of the currencies involved. In order to monitor the system, the International Monetary Fund (IMF) was founded in Washington and each country was obliged to fix its currency either against gold or against the US$ (itself tied to a gold price of $ 35 an ounce until 1971). Although the exchange rate could be adjusted, this was only possible under conditions of so-called 'fundamental economic imbalances' and not at the discretion of any specific government. Each exchange rate adjustment had to be approved by the IMF and/or those countries represented on the IMF's board. This framework was strong enough to give the system the necessary credibility and to keep it functioning until the start of the 1970s and indeed the IMF still performs an important role in world monetary affairs. In the 1950s and 1960s, BRETTON WOODS, helped by a relatively stable monetary environment, created an important basis for the global economic upswing after World War II.

The system started to falter in the late 1960s, when the USA began to pursue an expansive monetary policy chiefly to finance the Vietnam war. The excess supply of

---

[1]	An excellent overview of modern exchange rate history is given in R.I. Mc Kinnon's 'The Rules of the Game: International Money in Historical Perspective', Journal of Economic Literature, March 1993, pages 1–44.

dollars on the world markets caused by this and/or the exercising of the option by various central banks of exchanging paper money at a fixed rate against gold with the US Federal Reserve (the American central bank) when the USA had printed more dollars than were covered by gold reserves finally brought the system down. In mid-1971, therefore, gold convertibility had to be changed and then abandoned.

This meant that the system of fixed exchange rates, as defined at the BRETTON WOODS conference, was shaken to its very foundations. The hard currency countries – in particular Germany and Switzerland – were flooded with dollars, which in principle all had to be accepted by the central banks at a fixed rate. Since central banks had to pay for these dollars with domestic currency, this caused a massive rise in domestic money supply and inflation began to rise too. In the first half of the 1970s, both Germany and Switzerland did indeed display double-digit money supply growth rates and following this, double-digit inflation rates. In spring 1973, under the pressure of circumstances, it was decided to no longer support the US$ on the foreign exchange markets and to let the currencies float freely, ie. to let them find their own 'correct' exchange relationship according to supply and demand on the foreign exchange markets.

What remains to be added, a point referred to already, is that the early 1970s were characterised at several central banks, the Swiss and the German in particular, by the shift in emphasis of economic principle towards basic monetarist theory. Amongst these principles, the autonomous control of domestic money supply was given a decisive weight. Given such a new credo, it was not surprising that a de facto and de jure determination of domestic money supply by a foreign country (via the fixed exchange rate system) was not reconcilable with the prevailing 'Zeitgeist'. Without doubt, this led to an acceleration of the collapse of the Bretton Woods accord.

The 1970s transition to a floating exchange rate regime brought forth a veritable deluge of academic theses on the advantages and disadvantages of flexible exchange rates and their determinants. As already mentioned, the general tone of these papers was mostly optimistic. The expectation was that exchange rates would fluctuate in a relative stable manner around fundamental equilibrium levels although a possibly turbulent transition period might initially be seen. Another expectation was that speculation would play a somewhat stabilising role. In actual fact, events turned out rather differently. Within a very short period of time, the US dollar devalued dramatically but then, in the early 1980s, it staged an equally impressive climb to levels judged overvalued by almost every standard. Currencies generally developed an unexpected volatility, with massive and long-lasting deviations from widely accepted definitions of equilibria. The behaviour of various central banks was also not exactly what had been expected: several continued to intervene in the market but not so much to fix a rate as to smooth out short term fluctuations. In a number of

European countries this intervention was taken a step further with the formal establishment of the European Exchange Rate Mechanism (ERM) to operate something similar to Bretton Woods in a more limited European context. The US itself remained neutral as far as exchange rate developments were concerned and correspondingly held hardly any foreign exchange rate reserves. Other countries were free to pursue a domestic monetary policy and a domestic inflation target independent of the US.

For their part, academics had to overhaul their models relatively quickly after the initial dramatic experiences with flexible exchange rates and this gave rise to new theoretical approaches to exchange rate determination, the basic principles of which are still largely valid today. The decisive element was the insight that the foreign exchange market was no longer simply a market in which fluctuations of supply and demand arose when changes occurred in the flows of goods, for example import and export flows. Quite clearly, when international portfolios were rearranged, ie. when there were changes to international holdings of financial assets, this also had a dramatic effect on currency demand and therefore exchange rates. The incorporation of these new ideas into exchange rate theory will be discussed later in the next section. Suffice it to conclude here that what remains not so clear is the extent to which portfolio-related currency demand fluctuations have been exaggerated by the freedom from any restraint such as that imposed by a fixed exchange rate system (or capital movement constraints). However, recent experience suggests that central banks' attempts to impose restraints in the form of exchange rate stabilisation efforts might only be dwarfed by the massive scale of investors' portfolio movements, which are dependent on investors' opinions on where exchange rates are heading.

3. The fundamental determinants of exchange rate trends

Traditional methods of exchange rate determination were based on so-called size-of-flow considerations. In these cases, the argumentation went roughly like this: when – for example due to differing economic development – the import and export flows in two countries begin to drift apart, pressure starts to build up on the foreign exchange market, which either induces realignments in the exchange rate (with flexible rates) or intervention, which in turn tends to lead to adjustments in economic development.

To illustrate this, a simple example: let us assume that the US successfully manages to push ahead US economic growth by means of a particularly expansive monetary policy. Basically, in terms of the real economy, Switzerland would also benefit from this because the nascent demand for goods would lead to additional demand for US imports – and thus for Swiss exports. Assuming that the balance of trade and/or payments situation was in equilibrium, this would lead to a deficit in the US trade balance. Since US imports would normally be paid for in dollars, this would lead to an additional supply of US dollars on the foreign exchange market, as shown by the following graph.

The graph illustrates the supply and demand structures on the foreign exchange market which would ensue due to the trade flows.

Supply and demand structures on the foreign exchange market (flexible rates)

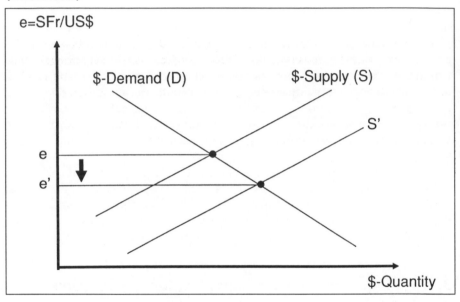

The SFr/US$ rates are shown on the vertical axis and the horizontal axis depicts the dollar flows on the foreign exchange market induced by the trade flows. The demand function (D) represents in this case the demand for dollars, which arises in Switzerland for payment of US exports and the supply function (S) shows how many dollars from the payment of Swiss exports to the USA flow into the market (Swiss exporters who receive payment for their goods in US$ will 'bring' these to the foreign exchange market in order to convert them into SFr).

If we now incorporate the expansive US economic policy into our conceptual model, we then get the following result: through the economically-induced excess demand for Swiss goods in the US (ie. the economically-induced US balance of trade deficit), there arises an excess supply of dollars on the foreign exchange market (S'). Given free price formation on the foreign exchange market, the consequence of this would be that the dollar would experience a devaluation from e to e' until such time as the balance of trade was in equilibrium again, because the value of Swiss goods has become greater for US consumers due to the devaluation of the dollar.

The value of the dollar, ie. the determinants of the exchange rate development, will in this model reflect all those (economic) variables, which influence both domestic and foreign economic growth, ie. in principle the whole set of economic data in the different countries; from money supply, interest rates and inflation to other economic variables such as consumer demand, unemployment and the government deficit and the balance of payments figures themselves. This is the 'traditional story' of flexible exchange rates.

With fixed exchange rates, the chain of argument runs differently of course and in this simple context, it can be shown that fixed rates lead to a much stronger 'tying together' of the different economies. 'Decoupling' of economies (variables such as domestic inflation and growth) is only possible with floating exchange rates.

With fixed exchange rates, the transmission of the expansive monetary impulse in the US into our model results in the following picture:

Supply and demand structure on the foreign exchange market (fixed rates)

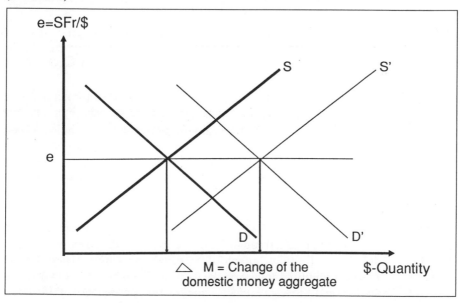

The accompanying excess supply of dollars (S') in this case does not simply lead to a devaluation but must be accommodated by additional demand (D'), so that the rate 'e' can remain unchanged. This additional demand can only be created by the central bank, which, in a fixed rate regime, is obliged to intervene whenever necessary on the foreign exchange market in order to keep the exchange rate stable. This leads to an increase in the foreign exchange reserves at (keeping to the case of our example) the Swiss National Bank. This foreign currency has to be paid for in SFr in the amount of (D'-D), which of course means nothing other than that the domestic money supply (M) has to be expanded by the same amount. In principle, however, this means that the original monetary impulse in the US has been translated into a monetary impulse in Switzerland due to the fixed exchange rate situation. Or in other words: in such a system, economic developments in different economies are irrevocably tied to each other for better or worse. Depending on the political and/or economic consensus and circumstances, this does not necessarily have to be a problem – as illustrated by the early success of the BRETTON WOODS era. With changes to the economic and/or monetary credo, however, problems can arise – as exemplified by the later collapse of the fixed rate system at the beginning of the 70s.

We have already pointed out in the introduction that the size-of-flow argumentation just described, which characterised the way of thinking in the 1950s and 1960s and which of course still has a certain importance today, is insufficient as an explanatory model to analyse exchange rate behaviour under a flexible regime. We know nowadays that hardly 10% of turnover on the foreign exchange market is induced by goods flows, the largest part by far comes from continuous reworking of international portfolios.

If this is the case, then the search for the fundamental determinants of the exchange rate must be based on a portfolio model, relegating to a minor role the size-of-flow way of thinking.

Portfolio-theoretical analyses of exchange rates are also based either implicitly or explicitly on some kind of equilibrium relationship or other – equilibrium relationships which are assumed to be valid (depending on the model used) at least in the long term.

Two of the most important equilibrium conditions in exchange rate theory are:

• Purchasing power parity
• Interest parity

The first of these two models implies in its simplest form that the exchange rate can be described as the equilibrating relationship between domestic and foreign price levels. In this case, we are talking about the so-called absolute interpretation of the purchasing power parity theory. In practice, however, the so-called relative interpretation is normally used, according to which the percentage change in the exchange rate can be explained roughly by the differences between the inflation rates of any two countries.

Basically, the purchasing power parity hypothesis can be derived from an analysis based on traditional goods arbitrage considerations but it can also be explained in an international portfolio context via the relationship between money and inflation.

The goods arbitrage model has already been sketched out above: put simply, internationally traded goods should cost the same at home and (after conversion at the exchange rate) abroad. If these prices deviate considerably, then goods arbitrage would have to be expected, which would influence both domestic and foreign prices and also the exchange rate. This – so the argumentation goes – would provide for a situation where, over the longer term, there would be a kind of equilibrium between the price trends in any two countries and the exchange rate of the currencies of these two countries. However, such price balance would only be valid for internationally traded goods and not for any random basket of goods or even for individual goods.[1]

An alternative derivation of the purchasing power parity hypothesis is based on the view that the exchange rate is something similar to the relative price of two currencies and every time that one currency loses value 'at home' due to domestic inflation, then its external value also falls. In other words, the currency of a high-inflation country will tend to devalue against the currency of a country with lower inflation. For example, if the US has a higher inflation level than Switzerland, then the dollar will tend to devalue and to roughly the extent of the inflation differential.

The following graph depicts one often-used way of representing the purchasing power parity theory in practice. It simultaneously shows both the development of the SFr/US$ rate from 1973 to 1993 and a so-called purchasing power parity band. Since the calculation of purchasing power parity is arbitrary to a certain degree, the concept of a band is often used and effective under- or overvaluation is only indicated as likely when the respective market rate leaves the band. Typically purchasing power parity is not seen as an instrument to be used for short-term exchange rate forecasting but it can provide an indication of the fundamental valuation of a currency. We will come back to this approach later in the section on investment policy conclusions.

---

[1] In this context, the recent attempt by the ECONOMIST to make a so-called 'Big Mac' parity popular as an indication of a fundamental over- or undervaluation of a currency is to be regarded more as a popular journalistic story than as a meaningful economic exercise.

Purchasing Power Parity
SFr/US$ since 1973

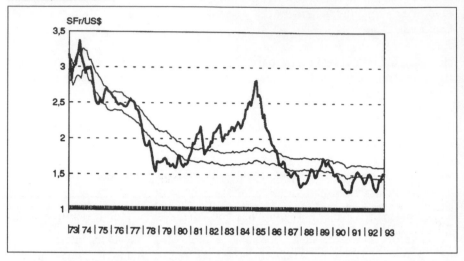

The graph does at least show that the tendency for inflation to be higher in the US than in Switzerland (the tendency for the purchasing power parity band to fall) has been accompanied by a trend-related (ie. long-term) devaluation of the dollar.

The second equilibrium concept – the interest rate parity theory – is sometimes shown in another form as an equation for determining the domestic interest rate. In the chapter on bonds we have already talked about this kind of approach. In its simplest form, the model states that the difference between domestic and foreign interest rates corresponds to the expected change in exchange rates (uncovered interest rate parity). An alternative formulation, which in principle represents nothing other than an arbitrage condition, states that the percentage difference between the spot and forward rate corresponds to the interest differential (covered interest rate parity). In the following we will look at a simple example which shows us why covered interest rate parity is an arbitrage condition.

The assumptions, on which our example is based, are the following: SFr/$ spot rate 1.40, SFr/$ forward rate in one year 1.50, interest rate on a 12 month horizon in Switzerland 4% (we assume that we can both invest and borrow at this rate), interest rate in the US on a 12 month horizon 10% (here also the same rate for investments and borrowings). It is obvious that the 10% interest rate in the US is interesting from the SFr investor's viewpoint and he therefore adopts the following strategy: he borrows SFr 140 000 from a Swiss bank at 4%, converts this into $ 100 000 and reinvests it at 10% in the US. The investor knows that in one year he will receive $ 110 000. He also knows that the forward rate is SFr/$ 1.50, ie. if he sells his $ 110 000 forward today, then he will get back a guaranteed SFr 165 000 in 12 months' time. The following table shows the corresponding money flows and the certain arbitrage profit of SFr 19 400 that this transaction secures for the investor.

	today	in 12 months
Borrowing at 4%	+ 140 000 SFr	– 145 600 SFr
Investment in $ at 10%	– 100 000 $	110 000 $
Forward sale of the 110 000 at 1.50	+ 165 000 SFr	

Risk-free profit SFr 165 000 – 145 600 = 19 400

Something in this calculation cannot be right. Whenever absolutely risk-free profits are possible in markets, somewhere a price is somehow wrong. Thinking through the example, it becomes immediately clear that either the difference in interest rates or the difference between spot and forward rates is wrong. In countries with free capital markets and currency convertibility, whenever there are sizeable discrepancies between the difference in interest rates on the one hand, and difference between spot and forward rates on the other, there will always be arbitrage activity in the sense described above. These arbitrage flows will only cease – ie. equilibrium will be reached – when the discrepancy between spot and forward rates for the respective time periods corresponds more or less exactly with the difference between the corresponding interest rates. The only reason for small deviations from this equilibrium will be due to factors such as transaction costs and adjustment lags (which can for all practical purposes be ignored here). The simple example given above should be sufficient to show that the 'covered interest rate parity' is indeed a pure arbitrage condition.

What is the theoretical consequence of covered and uncovered interest rate parity? Covered interest parity can be (approximately) described by the following formula:

(4.1.) $$\frac{F_t - E_t}{E_t} = i_t^* - i_t$$

where F describes the forward rate and the E the spot rate at the point in time t, i is the domestic interest rate and i* the corresponding foreign interest rate. In contrast, uncovered interest rate parity can be (approximately) formulated as follows:

(4.2.) $$\frac{E_{t+1}^e - E_t}{E_t} = i_t^* - i_t$$

Here E^e_{t+1} describes the expected exchange rate for the period t+1 at the time t.

Looking at the two equations, it becomes evident that as both equations must obviously be valid, the forward rate must correspond with the expected future spot rate. This assumption has often been used for testing the hypothesis of whether or not the forward rate is a good predictor of the future spot rate. It has been shown that in many cases the forward rate is not in fact a good predictor of the future spot rate, however, it is still the best available market estimate.[1]

Based on the two equilibrium hypotheses of purchasing power parity and interest rate parity, we will now attempt within the framework of a kind of portfolio model not only to derive the fundamental determinants of the exchange rate but also to say something about the short-term dynamics of exchange rate movements.

The following arguments may seem excessively theoretical to those not used to working with technical terms and readers who are not interested in the formal derivation can skip the next couple of pages to the point, where we have attempted to formulate the conclusions in 'normal language'. Nevertheless, we suggest that useful insights can be gained by working through the derivations even if this requires some effort.

In principle, the fundamental determinants can be derived from a money market equilibrium condition combined with the purchasing power parity hypothesis:

The domestic and foreign money demand functions[2] are designated by:

(4.3.) $m^d_t = a + p_t + by_t - ci_t + ...$

(4.3') $m^{d*}_t = a + p^*_t + by^*_t - ci^*_t + ...$

Here m^d, m^{d*} describe the demand for money at home and abroad, p describes the corresponding price trend, y the economic development and i the interest rate trend in the domestic market (without *) and abroad (variables with *). a, b and c are model parameters.

---

[1] See eg MEESE, R.A./ROGOFF, K.: 'Emprical Exchange Rate Models of the Seventies: Do they Fit Out-Of-Sample?', Journal of International Economics, 1983, Volume 14, p. 3–24, or HERI, E.W.: 'Market Efficiency and Forecasting: An Investigation of Foreign Exchange Markets', International Review of Economics and Business, 1986, Volume 3, p. 1057-76.

[2] For the sake of simplicity, the functions are specified logarithmically and the assumption is made that the domestic and foreign money demand elasticities are the same. All this simplifies the equations but does not detract from the basic assertions.

The equations signify that the amount of money (cash) held by the public is dependent on price, economic and interest rate developments as well as an unknown number of additional specific factors (shown by points), not included in this simplified formulation. We will come back to the importance of such possible additional variables later.

At the same time, we assume so-called permanent money market equilibrium:

(4.4) $\qquad m_t^s = m_t^d = m_t$

(4.4') $\qquad m_t^{s*} = m_t^{d*} = m_t^*$

which means that the money supply made available by the central banks in both countries does indeed correspond to the respective amount of money demanded (thus we can eliminate the clumsy use of s and d for supply and demand).

Furthermore, we introduce a simple formula for purchasing power parity,

(4.5) $\qquad e_t = p_t - p_t^*$

If we now solve the demand functions (4.3, 4.3') for the prices

$$p_t = m_t - a - by_t + ci_t - \dots$$

$$p_t^* = m_t^* - a - by_t^* + ci_t^* - \dots$$

and put these expressions using (4.4, 4.4') into the purchasing power parity formula (4.5), then we obtain:

(4.6) $\qquad e_t = (m_t - m_t^*) + b\,(y_t^* - y_t) + c\,(i_t^* - i_t) + \dots$

or in other words, the exchange rate is shown to be dependent on the monetary policy at home (m) and abroad (m*), – ie. on the relative development of monetary aggregates of the two respective countries – and on the relative economic trend and the relative interest rate development. Furthermore, many other variables play a role (in [4.6] again represented by points), although they do not receive specific mention in simplified formulations of the money demand function (cf. [4.3]).[1]

---

[1] Just a remark in passing that when using a wealth parameter in the money demand function for the two countries, the balance of payments again indirectly finds its way into the exchange rate equation.

The exchange rate equation (4.6) shows that the fundamental determinants of the exchange rate in a monetarist/portfolio theoretic model such as this are really not all that different from those which we derived, more directly but perhaps more contentiously, from the original trade (size-of-flow) models, ie. monetary policy, general economic developments and interest rates etc.

Equations such as (4.6) actually offer empirically testable hypotheses of exchange rate determination. Indeed such equations have been examined very thoroughly with regard to their explanatory power and also their forecasting ability[1]. In this context, it has been shown that in certain periods different variables seem to have more importance than in other periods. The derived structures are generally relatively unstable and the practical relevance of the equations is correspondingly limited.

If this is the case, then the next question we have to pose is whether this is attributable to the fact that the fundamental explanatory variables indicated above are, in fact, irrelevant or whether the way in which the influence of economic variables on the exchange rate is brought into the model should be questioned. The systematic incorporation into the model of the second equilibrium relationship – interest rate parity – does indeed offer a considerably deeper and probably more realistic insight into the way in which the derived economic variables have an influence on the exchange rate. It will also make it possible for us to show why statistical tests of equations like (4.6) lead to rather disappointing results.

If, in our exchange rate equation (4.6), we replace the interest rate term $[c(-it)]$ by the expected change in the exchange rate using the uncovered interest rate parity condition (4.2), then we obtain:

$$(4.7) \qquad e_t = (m_t - m_t^*) + b\,(y_t^* - y_t) + c\,(e_{t+1}^e - e_t) + \dots$$

where $(-et)$ describes the exchange rate fluctuation expected in the next period. The exchange rate then becomes dependent not only on the fundamental variables as derived from the corresponding money demand function, but also on the expected exchange rate fluctuation itself. If we now, for simplicity's sake, indicate the development of all fundamental variables by z_t, ie.

$$z_t = (m_t - m_t^*) + b\,(y_t^* - y_t) + \dots$$

---

[1] Cf. e.g. HERI, E.W.: Determinanten kurzfristiger Wechselkursfluktuationen, Hamburg 1992, or again MEESE, R.A./ROGOFF, K., 1983, loc.cit. or HERI, E.W., 1986, loc.cit.

then we can obtain the following expression for the exchange rate:

$$(4.8) \qquad e_t = \frac{1}{1+c} z_t + \frac{c}{1+c} e^e_{t+1}$$

If, however, the exchange rate in period t is dependent on the development of the fundamental variables (z) in period t and on the exchange rate expected in the next period, then it is equally correct that the rate expected in the next period is itself again dependent on the expected development of the fundamental parameters for the next period, and additionally on the exchange rate expected in the next period but one. If this substitution argument is 'shifted forward indefinitely', then we arrive at the following expression:

$$(4.9) \qquad e_t = \frac{1}{1+c} \sum_{k=0}^{\infty} \frac{c}{(1+c)^k} z^e_{t+k}$$

or more simply

> SFr/$ = function of all expected future developments in the fundamental economic variables in Switzerland and in the USA.

The expression for the exchange rate looks quite complex and all encompassing! The interpretation is however very interesting and is similar to the 'forward-looking' price models established for bonds and equities. For instance, the equation indicates that today's exchange rate already incorporates information on all present and future events which could be relevant for the exchange rate so that any changes expected in the explanatory variables (z) are accounted for. Correspondingly, the exchange rate will only change when something unexpected happens to change our future outlook.

A consequence is that remarks made by a central bank governor in respect of monetary policy in one year's time might, for example, move the exchange rate today because this might change the expectations 'contained' in today's exchange rate regarding monetary policy. Using such models, a whole series of exchange rate reactions which are sometimes far too quickly written off as being completely irrational becomes understandable. While the public in general often assumes a clear link between certain fundamental variables and the exchange rate – a frequent example is the expectation that the dollar will rise when dollar interest rates are on the increase – the model above shows that this reaction is by no means certain. If rising interest rates are expected and are in this sense already 'contained in the dollar', then an effective interest rate increase which turns out to be lower than expected can lead, quite rationally, to a fall in the dollar.

If this approach to exchange rate analysis is correct and the markets react rapidly and without delay to new information, then exchange rates – in the short term at least – should fluctuate more or less haphazardly. In fact, the erratic fluctuation of exchange rates has often been described as a 'Random Walk', a concept already discussed in the chapter on equities and to which we will return shortly.

We can summarise the observations made above regarding the fundamental determinants of exchange rates in a less formal manner:

One of the major components of exchange rate theory is purchasing power parity. At least implicitly based on this model, equations for the determination of exchange rates have been developed which show us in a relatively detailed way what the fundamental driving forces of exchange rate movements are. Without claiming to be complete, these are

- monetary policy
- economic activity
- interest rates
- inflation expectations and
- the balance of payments situation

in two respective countries.

The fundamental determinants, which are practically all of an economic or economic policy nature, appear to be rather clear. What is not quite clear – at least what does not emerge from the simpler approaches to exchange rate determination – is the way in which this influence is exercised, at least as far as the short-term dynamic is concerned. Here it has been shown that the influence operates mainly at the expectations level. It is not so much the change in a specific variable at the point in time t which is relevant but rather the effect this change has on the expectation structure. Since it can be assumed that in the markets every piece of relevant information is 'included in the price' at any one moment in time – in this context we talk about 'efficient markets' – new information will only come into the markets by chance and influence prices in a correspondingly random way. The result of this is that the very short-term dynamic of exchange rate trends more or less loses its economic interpretation, so that the economist will tend to concentrate more on longer-term, fundamental developments.

In the following table, we have attempted by way of an example to summarise the respective fundamental influences on the SFr/US$ exchange rate.

**Fundamental factors influencing
the SFr/US$ exchange rate**

	Direction	Influence
Monetary Policy CH USA	⬆⬆ (expansive)	⬆⬇
Economic activity CH USA	⬆⬆	⬇⬆
Real interest rate CH USA	⬆⬆	⬇⬆
Inflation expectations CH USA	⬆⬆	⬆⬇
Trade balance CH USA	Deterioration Improvement	⬇⬆

Nominal interest rate: the effect is basically dependent on whether the change is attributable to changes in real interest rates or to changes in inflation expectations.

The table provides a diagrammatic overview of the fundamentally expected medium-term exchange rate fluctuations which arise due to changes to the economic environment. In this context, the respective arrows are always to be understood 'ceteris paribus', ie. it is assumed that the changes always occur in otherwise unchangeable basic conditions (in other words that the other variables remain constant). As we can understand from the previous discussion about the price forming mechanism, the respective short-term actual fluctuation can easily be different from that fundamentally justified (as shown in the table). The short-term movement will always be dependent on what is already expected in the markets. It is therefore important to distinguish clearly here between long-term fundamental trends and short-term aberrations.

The table shows that a more expansive monetary policy in the US than in Switzerland tends to weaken the dollar (first line). We expect the opposite from a stronger economy on the other side of the Atlantic than in Switzerland (third line), and from higher real US interest rates (fifth line). The real interest rate argument arises in particular from the increasing attractiveness of direct investments with rising real interest rates and not necessarily from portfolio switches triggered by this, as will be discussed below. Increasing inflation expectations, on the other hand, tend to weaken a currency. This has firstly to do with monetary policy because inflation expectations are often raised in the wake of expansive monetary policy, but also has to do with the purchasing power parity argument, which states that a currency tends to change in line with the inflation differential vis-à-vis a foreign country. Furthermore, the table contains information on the trade balance, for which it is assumed that an improvement (in the US) would lead to a stronger dollar. This assumption is based on the size-of-flow argument, according to which an excess demand for dollars tends to arise when (US) exports exceed (US) imports. In connection with the US trade deficits of the mid-80s, we have learnt that this link is basically correct but that it is generally obscured, or over-ridden, by a number of other effects which makes it extremely difficult to actually filter out and identify empirically.

With nominal interest rates, we again get some interesting and partly contradictory information. It is of course by no means clear that rising nominal interest rates (even independently of the expectation structure!) automatically lead to an appreciation of a currency, as is often maintained. In actual fact, it is more likely to be the case that those countries with the highest nominal interest rates also have the strongest devaluation rates. Normally, however, it is the inflation rate and/or inflation expectations which are responsible for the high nominal interest rates and thus also for the devaluation. In each individual case, it is therefore very important to know whether a change in nominal interest rates is attributable to changes in real interest rates or to a change in the inflation mentality of an economy. Thus, given increasing interest rates in the US, the dollar could fundamentally rise or fall. It should by no means be regarded as an irrationality of the market when, given increasing interest rates, the dollar rises in one phase and falls in another. Depending on the particular economic environment under which interest rate changes occur, other effects on the currency are to be expected.

These observations already point in the direction of certain conclusions regarding investment policy which will be outlined below.

4. Conclusions for investment policy

We have already indicated that exchange rate considerations in investment policy are an important issue in Europe, probably because internationally diversified portfolios are more commonly held than in the US. However, there is no doubt that the 'internationalisation' of investment policy is also reaching the US. Points highlighting this are: stronger emphasis on risk aspects of portfolio management, recognition of the fact that markets are not perfectly correlated internationally, creating the opportunity to reduce risk by international diversification and finally recognition of the fact that certain foreign markets are obviously more resistant to various exogenous shocks than the domestic market itself. Because of this increasing interest in 'internationalisation' and its 'benefits', some of the more pragmatic problems for an international investment policy will be tackled in the following sections.

4.1 Long-term equilibria

It is clearly recognised that not only is it difficult to forecast short term exchange rate changes, but also it is often difficult to give a reason for such changes, even after the event. The last section introduced a possible explanation for this troublesome phenomenon. But it is possible that the equilibrium relationships used in theory could provide at least an indication of long-term exchange rate trends. This brings us back to the subject of purchasing power parity.

Long-term equilibria have already kept armies of economists occupied for decades. For example, the following graph can be found in John Maynard Keynes' book 'Tract on Monetary Reform', from 1923

Theory of money and the exchanges

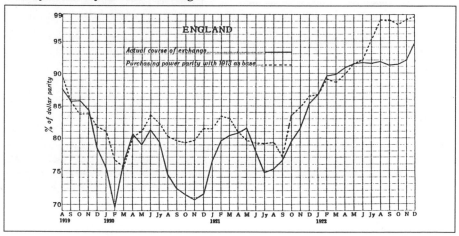

The graph shows the development of the £/$ rate from 1919 to 1923 and the corresponding development of purchasing power parity as calculated by Keynes seen as something of a 'fundamental anchor' for the development of exchange rates. But what are these indicators used for? During the period of floating exchange rates since 1973, Swiss Bank Corporation has calculated a number of purchasing power parity rates which we have been able to utilise as an example here. The following purchasing power parity graphs can be interpreted in a similar way to the chart in

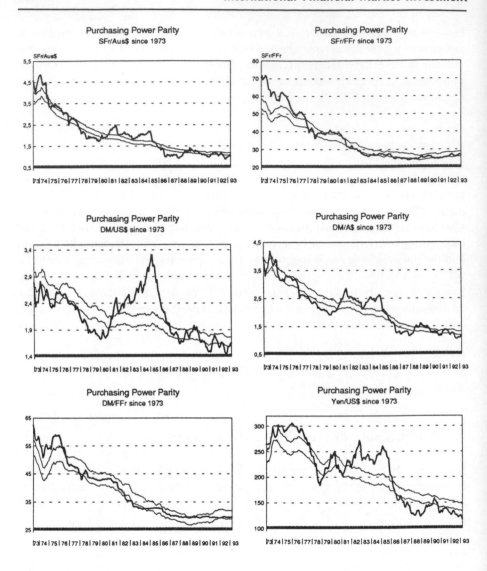

section 3. The calculations are based on the development of the respective wholesale price indices and on the (empirical) observation that the deviation of effective rates from purchasing power parity can be approximated by a delayed adjustment process, ie. a so-called 'stable AR(2) process'[1]. It is clear, of course, that the real exchange rate is not constant (which would imply strict validity of purchasing power parity).

However, it can be assumed that the equilibrium value calculated from purchasing power parity provides at least a reasonable point of reference which can be used to indicate in some way extremes of over- and under-valuation, eg Autumn 1978 for the Swiss Franc, year-end 1984/85 [overvaluation] and 1987/88 [under-valuation] for the US dollar, and late 1988 for the overvaluation of the pound sterling versus the DM.

On the one hand, such indicators can be used to judge whether interest rate differentials between countries offer interesting investment opportunities once potential changes in exchange rates are taken into account – this subject will be discussed in more detail in the next section. On the other hand, purchasing power parity can be used to put hedging strategies on a fundamental footing. For example, an importer of US-made products faced with a strongly rising dollar may no longer wish to buy all his dollars at the forward rate, especially if he can see that the dollar is becoming over-valued, say by as much as 30% (spring 1985). Because he believes that the dollar is more likely to return to its equilibrium value in the longer term, he will try not to tie himself into what is seen as a 'fundamentally false rate' in the forward market over such a long time. In such a case, he would be likely to consider options strategies, at least for part of his requirements to limit his exposure to currency fluctuations. This could allow him, for instance, to obtain dollars at approximately the current rate should the US currency continue to rise, or at a favourable rate should the dollar fall. Even here, some guide to fundamental equilibrium rates can be of help, even though they will not be able to replace a proper hedging strategy.

4.2 Interest rate differentials and exchange rate risk

It has already been pointed out briefly that a higher interst rate often makes the corresponding currency in a particular country 'a priori' seem more attractive, at least before investigating all the possible hidden reasons behind the high interest rates.

In fact, from this point of view of monetary and currency theories, large interest rate differentials are often relatively simple to explain. In many cases, they stem from the policy positions of central banks and are influenced by the relative economic situations. Despite the risks, many international investors see such differences in interest rates as offering a chance of additional income. The argument proceeds in

---

[1]   This simply indicates a particular form of lag structure in the equation (indicating delayed adjustment of the exchange rate to its theoretic value). For a more detailed description of the methods see HOLZER, S./ NOORLANDER, J.: 'Purchasing Power Parity, the SBC Approach in the SBC Global', March 1991.

this way: if a foreign bond with a (time to) maturity of ten years yields, say, eight percentage points more interest than a domestic paper of a similar quality and maturity, then the corresponding currency could lose more than 50% of its actual value over the whole maturity, and the foreign investment would still be equivalent or on a 'par' with a domestic investment. As such a large change in exchange rates may seem unlikely, at least in the short-run, foreign investments seem to promise a relatively risk-free additional yield. Tables showing interest rate differentials can be simply calculated – examples can be seen in the financial press. They indicate for the investor in a foreign market how much he could see an exchange rate fall and still receive the same overall sum on expiry as if he had left the money in his home market. The results are sometimes, inaccurately, described in the economic press as 'exchange rate risk'.

It should be clear from the previous discussions why this is inaccurate. Firstly we know that the difference in interest rates in the usual definition does not measure or describe 'exchange rate risk', but the change in the (equilibrium) exchange rate which is objectively to be expected given current information. A higher nominal interest rate abroad in many cases reflects the fact that monetary and fiscal policies are conducted differently from country to country. According to long term trends, a higher nominal interest rate tends to go hand in hand with a higher rate of inflation and, from the arguments on purchasing power parity, even with an expected devaluation of the foreign currency.

'Risk' therefore exists less in the sense that the exchange rate will be devalued according to the interest rate differential – one must allow for this objectively – but more in the sense that the exchange rate, including the rate on maturity, may deviate massively from this expected long-term equilibrium.

Therefore, it should not simply be a case of commenting on and interpreting interest rate differentials. The interpretation must always address both the current level of interest rates and possible deviations of exchange rates from any defined equilibrium – eg purchasing power parity.

The second point to be discussed here is less concerned with the expected change in exchange rates, but more with the 'average behaviour' of investors, who have all been attracted by obvious interest rate differentials. The usual interest rate tables are based on one of the 'Zero Bond arguments', meaning that it is assumed that annual coupon payments can be regularly reinvested at the original interest rate. The same problem arises here as that dealt with in the concept of maturity yields, discussed in the chapter on bonds. Apart from the fact that foreign interest rates are highly unlikely to remain permanently fixed at the same level, the assumption of reinvestment does not realistically assume that – with the exception of professionally managed portfolios – not only will annual interest payments not be reinvested at the original interest rates, but that the 'happy event' of the interest rate payment will be used as an opportunity to use up at least a part of the capital for normal consumer activities (holidays, Christmas presents, tax payments etc.). Indeed, the individual behaviour of investors often provides a simple argument as to why the difference in interest rates is more likely to lead to unpleasant, as opposed to pleasant, surprises in international investments. Comments such as: particularly large differences in interest rates offer '..... a comfortable currency cushion', '....here the risk-conscious investor can be fully aware of the currency risk', simply do not correspond with the reality of floating exchange rates.

4.3 Real versus nominal interest rates

As a rule, a discussion on real interest rates cannot properly take place in the context of international investment opportunities, but rather in connection with domestic opportunities. It can be argued – as in the section on bonds – that an investor is basically not interested in the nominal yield of an investment – the nominal coupon in the case of bonds – but in 'what he can buy with the coupon payment', ie. the **real** yield.

Real interest rates can be defined in many different ways. A usual formula is to subtract the actual inflation rate from the nominal interest rate (ex post real interest rate). This definition is very simple to calculate from known statistics. However, it does not allow for the fact that in principle, the present inflation rate is no longer the relevant rate for an investor, because the yield only falls due in a future period. Correspondingly, this must be deflated with a future – expected – inflation rate. This leads to the definition of the 'ex ante real interest rate', calculated using the expected inflation rate over the period of interest. As expected values of national economic data are estimated only with uncertainty, the ex post real interest rate is generally a much more popular concept than the ex ante rate. However, this should not be allowed to obscure the fact that ex ante real interest rates are naturally the more relevant concept for investors. Both concepts are identical if, and only if, the expected inflation rate corresponds with the actual present rate.

A further nuance in the discussion of real interest rates is the international concept. In many cases, comparisons of real interest rates are made alongside comparisons of nominal interest rates on international investments. It is often argued that investments could be more interesting in those countries with particularly high **real** interest rates. Such an argument could be relevant when making direct investments (eg constructing a factory abroad, etc.). However, it is of lesser importance when making pure financial investments. The nominal yield gained through investment in any market will be consumer-relevant in the home market, not abroad, so that in principle the foreign real interest rate (defined as foreign nominal interest rate minus expected foreign rate of inflation) should not be considered a useful concept. What is relevant is the **foreign nominal yield (in domestic currency) minus the domestic rate of inflation.** The only way in which the foreign real yield becomes meaningful here is if this affects the exchange rate outlook in some way, a different consideration entirely. Even though this may amount to the same thing in long-term equilibrium (purchasing power parity!), it is yet another example of the fact than in many analyses the (possible) relevance of the coupon yield (in the case of bonds) is not taken into account. It also shows that it makes sense to consider precisely the final aim of the investment, which currency should be used and which risk preferences are involved, before investing in any currency for any type of security.

Chapter 5

The Theory of Efficient Markets

Having mentioned this subject from time to time in previous chapters, we should at least cover, albeit briefly, the basic concepts and controversy surrounding the theory. The theory of efficient markets is based on the assumption that all market participants know all relevant price information at any time and therefore react to any new announcements in such a way that prices instantaneously and permanently 'include' this information. If this were truly the case, then it would no longer be possible to outperform the stockmarket by adopting a stock-picking approach using public information and analysis of any kind (eg a fundamental review or technical chart) but outperformance would be purely a matter of chance, like rolling dice. Indeed, the same impossibility of outperformance would be true for other financial instruments (bonds, foreign exchange holdings etc.). Furthermore, the theory implies that prices would only react to unexpected events (everything known and expected has already been accounted for in the price), and they would therefore exhibit random fluctuations.

It becomes clear that under the theory of efficient markets, we are assuming a type of information and behaviour theory which implies the use by investors of pricing models already discussed in the previous chapters. But what information is used by participants in the markets for pricing, and in what way? We will come back to this question shortly.

Under the assumption of efficient markets, the so-called 'random walk hypothesis' becomes important. What does this mean for asset prices? Ask most analysts, or investors, to estimate the expected average annual rise in the stockmarket, and most will make an estimate based on an indicative market interest rate plus a risk premium (the interest rate itself being based, at least in the medium-term, on inflation plus a premium). This simply refers back to the basic notions of capital market equilibrium: financial assets must offer 'suitable' relative recompense. We need not go into further detail here, but clearly what is meant by an asset price following a 'random walk' is actually a process of unpredictable price deviations from this equilibrium rising trend[1].

The efficient market hypothesis has been tested for all financial markets (bonds, equities, exchange rates), both theoretically and empirically. In fact, quite a lot of evidence has been put together which agrees in general with the theory of efficiency, and with the random walk concept.

Empirical research tends to approach the issue by defining three different types of efficiency, differing only in the amount of information assumed to be available and assimilated in the market:

---

[1] See MALKIEL, B.: 'A random walk down Wall Street', Norton 1973 (paperback 1991).

- **Weak efficiency:** This concerns the question of whether or not the **information contained in past price developments** is reflected in the current price, or in other words, whether any opinions on future price developments can be deduced from patterns in past price developments. Do price patterns repeat or not? This type of efficiency is naturally a direct challenge to technical analysis, which explicitly assumes information related to the future is contained in past price developments. The theory of efficiency sets technical analysis against the random walk theory. Empirical research into the random walk hypothesis leaves no doubt about the fact that most financial market prices exhibit a more or less random pattern in the short-term. However, such results cannot indiscriminately be seen as equivalent to a falsification of chart techniques, as the statistical procedures usually used for testing weak efficiency are based on linear concepts, while chart techniques in many cases assume – at least implicitly – non-linear processes. However, it has already been pointed out that many of the hypotheses derived from chart analysis cannot in principal be falsified at all.

- **Semi-strong efficiency**:   Here we ask not just whether all the information contained in past price behaviour has been 'included' in the current price, but also whether **all publicly available information** has already been accounted for. In this context, 'publicly available' means information published in the media or in annual reports of companies and/or national economies, etc. It is clear that given this definition of efficiency, fundamental analysis as a method of price forecasting is also called into question. Numerous empirical investigations tend to show convincing evidence in favour of the efficiency hypothesis. But even here, there are similar caveats to those quoted above regarding statistical methods. It is frequently the case that time lags occur between 'new' announcements and recognition of incorrectly valued shares, although this is not supposed to happen in 'perfect' markets.

- **Strong efficiency**:   This concerns not just publicly available information, but all information relevant to the markets – including 'inside information'. It is hardly surprising that this strong type of market efficiency cannot as a rule be empirically tested or confirmed.

The theory of efficient markets suggests, quite plausibly, that most financial market prices exhibit an approximate random walk, ie. erratic characteristics, and are extraordinarily difficult to forecast. In contrast to statements often made, this is in no way a declaration of bankruptcy for the analysis of financial markets. Quite the contrary: complete market efficiency is the final consequence of fully efficient information processing. Only when information is efficiently and sensibly processed in the markets do the results described above arise. Also, efficiency does not necessarily mean that it is impossible in an individual case to achieve outperformance with the help of systematic research. Indeed, some successful investors have written books on this topic, describing the careful and detailed research they undertook prior to investment. However, it is difficult to prove, or disprove, whether their success was luck or judgement which can be repeatedly applied. Fundamental analysts are usually quite willing to admit that they have little chance of short-term outperformance, but they do claim that in the longer-term fundamental value will prevail, that is companies with continuously good track records see their shares outperform. In this case, concentration is on forecasting the longer-term trend about which short term random deviations may indeed occur. Detailed research and methodology which is not easily accessible to all investors, may even be considered a form of asymmetric information, or, in a way, 'insider' information (although not necessarily of the form usually implied when this phrase is used ie. in the legal sense). It is difficult to imagine all forms of inequality, and information cost, being eliminated thus markets will be less than perfect in the real world.

The use of any forecasts obviously creates risks. The efficiency theory in this context implies that an investor could be led into taking excessive risks by supposedly successful 'Gurus'. If the probability of being right (in direction) is only fifty/fifty – as in the case of the random walk – then the chance that someone could be right four times in succession, even by sheer accident, is one in sixteen, which seems quite high.

The following chart provides some indication of the problems of forecasting:

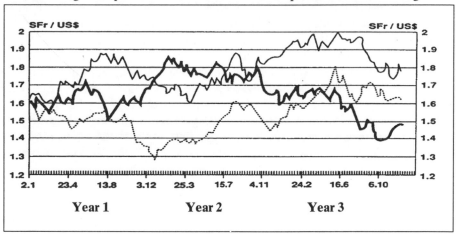

The chart shows the development of three time series (monthly values) over a period of three years. One of these lines is the SFr/US$ exchange rate. The other two have been artificially generated by drawing numbers at random (from a distribution with similar properties to the distribution of the exchange rate changes). It is left to the reader himself to determine which line depicts the real dollar development, and which the artificially generated time series. However, there is no doubt that the behaviour of all the time series appear rather similar.

The above example has been calculated using the SFr/US$ exchange rate, but the same could be done using any financial market price. As we have already explained in the section on exchange rates, such a more or less arbitrary behaviour of prices is not necessarily an expression of irrational behaviour, but can be fundamentally explained within the framework of the efficient market hypothesis. Pricing models show that the short-term price fluctuations may be driven by nothing other than rapid (efficient) revisions of expectations based on essentially unpredictable new information (see equation (4.6) in the exchange rate chapter).

If the theory of efficient markets is generally accepted by an investor as relevant in practice then this suggests that he should adopt a purely passive investment strategy. Such an investment strategy accepts that there are no recognisable and exploitable inefficiencies in markets and outperformance would occur only by chance. In terms of stockmarkets, this also means choosing an optimum equity portfolio, consisting in principle of all shares in the market, ie. holding a so-called 'index portfolio'. This type of question will be discussed again in more detail in the following chapter.

For many, particularly professional institutional investors, this conclusion drawn from market efficiency theory goes too far. These investors perhaps have more opportunity to profit from the slightest inefficiencies in markets. Accordingly, much literature has been produced dealing intensively with very specific forms of inefficiency and the possibility of exploiting these.

Specific, perhaps rather trivial, examples which have been frequently quoted are the 'January effect', 'Small Company effect', 'Neglected firm effect', etc. Empirical evidence for or against such inefficiency in stockmarkets is at present mixed[1]. Furthermore, professional investors appear to have become increasingly involved in such issues in recent years. This is not surprising given the usual claim of such professionals to be able to enhance performance, in effect through a greater ability to spot inefficiencies and exploit them. The reasons for such claims (learning curves, imperfect information flows and processing, information and transaction costs, existing constraints on some investors, etc.) and evidence of their validity are rather beyond the scope of this book, but it is important that all investors are at least familiar with the broad issues.

---

[1]   For an overview of this literature, see COULSON, DR.: 'The Intelligent Investor's Guide to Profiting from Stock Market Inefficiencies', New York: Prolus 1987. For readers more inclined towards academic literature in this field: HOTZ, P.: 'Das Capital Asset Pricing Model und die Markteffizienzhypothese unter besonderer Berücksichtigung der empirisch beobachteten 'Anomalien' in den amerikanischen und anderen internationalen Aktienmärkten', Dissertation St. Gallen 1988.

Even for smaller portfolios there are potentially inefficiencies to be exploited. Examples readily come from some of the Continental European bond markets in which 'wrongly priced' bonds are often identified relatively easily. Instruments which are rather complex to analyse, such as dual currency bonds (mentioned briefly in chapter I), have tended to offer yields over and above those received from other bonds of the same quality. Inefficiencies of this type are, in general, open only to private investors, because in many cases there is not enough volume (paper) available in the markets to make such instruments interesting for institutional investors (which potentially explains why the inefficiency occurs in the first place, offering opportunities for the more able small investor!).

Thus, even when it is assumed that markets are on average relatively efficient (correct and rapid processing of information), there may remain inefficiencies which can be exploited. However, it might not be wise, or possible, to base an overall investment strategy exclusively on finding inefficiencies: these must be considered more as an addition to, rather than substitute for, a fully-diversified portfolio.

Chapter 6

Fundamentals of
Modern Portfolio Theory

1. Introduction

Some of the basic principles of pricing and risk analysis of individual securities have already been discussed in the previous chapters. The treatment of risk concepts is in response to the fact that investment management is increasingly regarded as some form of risk management. However, in no way does risk management mean that all risks should be avoided. It means that an investor must understand that a higher expected return in general is 'bought' only with higher risks, and how to deal with this professionally and systematically. This goes together with the requirement for (quantitative) risk measurement and pre-occupation with modern methods of risk limitation (portfolio structuring, hedging strategies, portfolio insurance, etc.). Modern portfolio theory provides the basic groundwork for such concepts.

We will begin this chapter by explaining some simple statistical methods for analysing the properties of portfolios, particularly the relationships between securities, before going on to show how such properties can be manipulated to produce enhanced and more coherent investment strategies.

2. Mean/variance analysis

It has been seen in earlier chapters that for most financial assets, historic variance and standard deviation are sensible statistical concepts of risk measurement. But as we are not looking at single assets but whole portfolios in this chapter, we must begin by defining how the expected return, or yield, and the risk of a portfolio are derived from the corresponding properties of the individual securities.

The **yield of a portfolio** presents no particular problem. It can simply be calculated as the weighted average of the yields of all the individual securities in the portfolio. The equation is given as follows:

$$(6.1) \qquad R_p = x_1 \ R_1 + x_2 \ R_2 + ... + x_n \ R_n \ = \ \sum_{i=1}^{n} \ x_i \ R_i$$

Ri stands for the return on the security i, x_i is the proportion of the total portfolio invested in security i, and R_p is the return on the total portfolio.

Here is a simple example: In the table below are the yields of five securities (i = 1 to 5) and the proportion of these assets held in the example portfolio:

Security (i)	Yield from i (R$_i$)	Proportion held in portfolio (x$_i$)
1	5%	0
2	10%	0.5
3	12%	0.5
4	18%	0
5	28%	0

The yield of this two-asset portfolio (nothing is actually held of securities 1, 4 and 5) is as follows:

$$R_P = 0.5 \ (10\%) + 0.5 \ (12\%) = 11\%$$

Determining the **total risk of a portfolio,** however, is somewhat more demanding. New statistical concepts must be introduced here, which provide information on how far the returns on individual equities 'concur' (ie. move in sympathy with each other). Technically speaking, we must examine the extent to which equity returns are **correlated**.

First of all we need to introduce the statistical term of 'co-variance', which provides relationship information on how far the return on Asset 2 (R_{2i}) is above average ($\bar{R}_2$) if the return on Asset 1 (R_{1i}) is above average ($\bar{R}_1$) in period i. The co-variance is some measure of this and is defined as follows:

(6.2) $$\sigma R_1 R_2 \ = \frac{1}{n-1} \ \sum_{i=1}^{n} (\bar{R}_{1i} - R_1) \ (\bar{R}_{2i} - R_2)$$

This again presents a similar problem to the variance discussed in the chapter on equities. It is difficult to interpret the units of co-variance. It is for this reason that co-variance is seldom referred to, but rather the relationship concept of 'correlation' is used in preference, although this is only calculated from the co-variance divided by the individual standard deviations. Correlation is defined as follows:

(6.3) $$\rho R_1 R_2 \ = \frac{\sigma R_1 R_2}{\sigma R_1 \ \sigma R_2}$$

According to the definition, the correlation will lie between -1 and +1, taking the same sign as the respective co-variance term, as we can see from the equation. A value for the correlation of +1 shows that the yields of the two particular securities are totally dependent on each other, ie. they behave in the same way and, indeed, for investment purposes, they can be treated as the same security. A value of -1 shows that they behave in contrarian fashion, ie. if one yield rises, the other falls. Lastly, a value of zero indicates that the yields of the two assets are totally independent from each other. In the following charts, we give two examples of correlated yields

Strong relationship

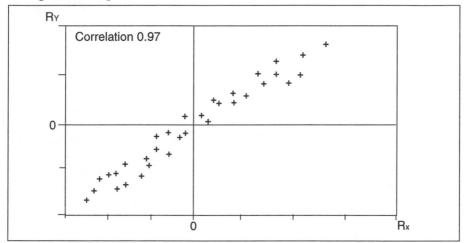

Weak relationship

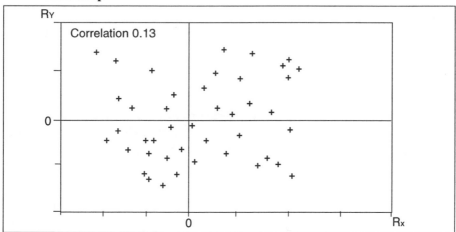

The yields of share Y are shown on the vertical axes; of share X on the horizontal axes. In the first graph, we illustrate the example of a high correlation close to 1, whilst in

the second, the correlation assumed is 0.13, close to zero (a weak relationship). The first graph should be interpreted as illustrating that high yields for share Y are consistent with high yields for share X, and vice versa, as might be the case if both shares were of companies in the same sector (eg. both chemical companies). The second graph illustrates the situation when yields have virtually no relationship with each other (eg. one share represents a large pharmaceutical company, the other a small builders merchant).

We now return to the measurement of risk (standard deviation) of a portfolio. Correlation, in fact, plays an important part here, as shown in the following definition of the risk measurement of a two-asset portfolio:

$$(6.4) \qquad \sigma p = \sqrt{x_1^2 \sigma_1^2 + x_2^2 \sigma_2^2 + 2x_1 x_2 \sigma_1 \sigma_2 \rho_{12}}$$

This expression is already relatively complex for two assets, and will become even more complicated as the number of assets held increases. If we want to calculate the risks for the portfolio shown in the above yield table, we obviously need estimates for the individual variances and co-variances for all five securities in question. In this example, the 'variance/co-variance matrix' (VCV-Matrix) takes the following form:

Variance/co-variance matrix

	1	2	3	4	5
1	4	2	1.5	3	3.2
2		6	**2.3**	3.2	3.4
3			**6**	2.8	1.7
4				8	2.1
5					8

The diagonal of this matrix shows the variances of the returns on the individual securities 1-5, ie. the individual risks, while the off-diagonal terms are the corresponding co-variances, as defined in equation (6.2). We already know, from the table showing the yields, that our portfolio actually comprises assets 2 and 3. Equation (6.4) therefore tells us that to determine the overall risk of this portfolio, we firstly need to determine the standard deviations of assets 2 and 3, together with the corresponding correlation.

From the VCV matrix, we get: $\qquad \sigma_2 = \sqrt{6} = 2.45$
$$\sigma_3 = \sqrt{6} = 2.45$$
$$\sigma_{23} = 2.3$$

This gives:

$$\rho_{23} = \frac{\sigma_{23}}{\sigma_2 \cdot \sigma_3} = \frac{2.3}{2.45 \cdot 2.45} = 0.38$$

And the portfolio risk accordingly becomes:

$$\sigma_p^2 = 0.5^2 \cdot 6 + 0.5^2 \cdot 6 + 2 \cdot 0.5 \cdot 0.5 \cdot 0.38 \cdot 2.45 \cdot 2.45 = 4.15$$

or:
$$\sigma_p = \sqrt{4.15} = 2.04$$

using the standard deviation.

The calculated variance of 4.15 for the portfolio is some 30% **less** than the variance of either of the individual assets, which – according to the VCV matrix – is 6 for both securities. In contrast, the yield of the portfolio is not reduced when compared with the individual asset's yields since the portfolio return is just a simple weighted average of the individual returns. It is already clear from this simple example that structuring a portfolio leads to a substantial reduction in risk as the yields of the assets involved usually show some correlation, but one which is less than unity. Indeed it would seem rather nonsensical from the point of view of investment strategy to hold a portfolio of two shares (or more) if these were perfectly correlated with each other (ie. correlation = 1). The shares would be perfect substitutes in terms of price performance. In this case a portfolio of only one share (arbitrarily chosen from the group of all perfectly correlated shares) would do just as well, having exactly the same characteristics as any combination of the shares in the group described. The whole point of holding several securities, rather than one, is clearly to 'gain' from diversification via reduced risk which comes from using the information given by the correlation patterns.

However, it is only possible to assess such gains when the information on the correlations is available. Thus a question we should also attempt to tackle is how to obtain estimates for the variance/co-variance matrix. It should always be remembered throughout the discussion that we can only ever operate with estimates for these important parameters and therefore these can be subject to error and may also change over time as relationships between the assets change. For example, if a company were to make a major change in its business orientation, its share price might exhibit a new relationship versus other company shares, ie. the co-variance matrix changes. Nevertheless, we must operate with statistical estimates for the terms in the VCV matrix which rely heavily on historical data[1].

---

[1] Clearly, one aim of fundamental analysis can be to provide judgemental revisions to such historical estimates. Technical analysis, of the more sophisticated kind, may also play a role here.

From the equations which defined the concepts of variance and co-variance, it is clear that a considerable amount of data is needed to calculate such parameters. If it is assumed that at least 30 data points are needed to reasonably calculate a single variance, then to calculate the above VCV matrix, at least 150 share price observations will be needed. Furthermore, these prices need to be corrected for dividends, share-splits, etc. (fortunately often done in specialist databases). Clearly an enormous amount of data is required for larger portfolios. This is only mentioned to illustrate the logistical problems posed. If investment management and investment counselling are understood to be a form of risk management, as indicated at the beginning of this chapter, then it becomes obvious that managers cannot avoid treating such concepts as variance and co-variance measurements, however difficult and demanding they may be. However, we should also point out that even in the absence of statistical data and techniques, an investor should be better able to make some assessment of a portfolio's properties given an understanding of the concept of interdependence.

It is clear from equation (6.4) that the variance, ie. the risk, for a portfolio is basically made up of two components: a group of terms relating to the 'average' risk of the individual assets, and a group of correlation terms which allows for the relationship between assets. A portfolio normally contains more than two assets, although we assumed this for simplicity in our example. The calculation of portfolio risk given an arbitrary number (n) of assets is made up of terms such as the ones in equation (6.4), and looks like this:

$$(6.5) \qquad \sigma^2_p = \sum_{j=1}^{n} x^2_j \cdot \sigma^2_j + \sum_{j=1}^{n} \sum_{\substack{k=1 \\ j \neq k}}^{n} x_j \, x_k \, \rho_{jk} \, \sigma_j \, \sigma_k$$

$$\underbrace{}_{\text{'Variance' term}} \quad \underbrace{}_{\text{'Correlation' term}}$$

When discussing the Capital Asset Pricing Model, a rather intuitive argument was used to show that only market risk (ie. systematic risk) as opposed to non-systematic risk (ie. company specific risk) will be 'rewarded'. The reason for this was that non-systematic risk can basically be eliminated by offsetting effects. This conclusion can also be derived with the help of equation (6.5). To show this we will use – for simplification – the assumption of equally weighted investments in the portfolio. In other words, it is assumed that all investments contained in a portfolio have the same weight x = 1/n, where n = the number of assets. Equation (6.5) then becomes[1]:

$$(i) \qquad \sigma^2_p = \frac{1}{n} \sum_j \frac{\sigma^2_j}{n} + \sum_j \sum_{\substack{k \\ j \neq k}} \left(\frac{1}{n}\right)^2 \sigma_{jk}$$

---

[1] For simplicity, equation (6.3) is used, substituting $\rho_{jk} \, \sigma_j \, \sigma_k$ by σ_{jk}

If the second summation term is multiplied by (n-1)/(n-1) and regrouped, then:

(ii) $$\sigma^2_p = \frac{1}{n} \sum_j \frac{\sigma^2_j}{n} + \frac{(n-1)}{n} \sum_j \sum_{\substack{k \\ j \neq k}} \frac{\sigma_{jk}}{n(n-1)}$$

Given the restriction 'j ≠ k', we have exactly n(n-1) co-variance terms in equation (ii), thus the summation part of the second term is equivalent to the average co-variance of the returns ($\bar{\sigma}_{jk}$) on the portfolio. In addition, the first summation term can be seen as the average variance ($\sigma^2_j/n = \bar{\sigma}^2_j$), so we can rewrite (ii) as:

(iii) $$\sigma^2_p = \frac{1}{n} \bar{\sigma}^2_j + \frac{n-1}{n} \bar{\sigma}_{jk}$$

It is obvious that increasing diversification, ie. an increasing number (n) of investments in a portfolio, decreases the variance (first) term. Indeed as n becomes larger, this variance term approaches zero.

The co-variance (second) term, in contrast, does not approach zero, but approaches the average co-variance.

$$\frac{(n-1)}{n} \sigma_{jk} \xrightarrow{n \to \infty} \bar{\sigma}_{jk}$$

All this can be defined in words in the following way: The risk of a portfolio basically consists of two (collected) terms, a variance term, which represents the 'average' risk of the individual securities in the portfolio, and a correlation or co-variance term, which defines the dependencies existing between the individual securities. It can be shown that as the number of securities in the portfolio increases (ie. n increases), the importance of the variance – ie. the individual risks – approaches zero (first term in above equation [iii]). Individual security risks, ie. **company specific risks, can therefore be virtually eliminated by diversification.** The correlation risks, ie. those which are market specific (systematic), on the other hand, will remain the same. For very large portfolios, the risk therefore corresponds to the average co-variance of all assets contained in the portfolio.

The following table contains a practical example of this diversification effect using shares listed on the New York Stock Exchange. Monthly data were used in the calculations which show an average variance of 46.619 with an average co-variance of 7.058. The table shows how the portfolio risk changes as the number of assets in the portfolio increases. Initially it equals the average variance of the particular security but it then moves closer to the average co-variance of the 1,000 securities[1].

---

[1]) The table originates from ELTON, E.Y./GRUBER, M.: 'Modern Portfolio Theory and Investment Analysis', New York: John Wiley & Sons, 1987 (3rd Edition).

Number of securities/Expected portfolio risk

Number of securities	Expected portfolio risk	Number of securities	Expected portfolio risk
1	46,619	75	7,585
2	26,839	100	7,453
4	16,948	125	7,374
6	13,651	150	7,321
8	12,003	175	7,284
10	11,014	200	7.255
12	10,354	250	7,216
14	9.883	300	7,190
16	9,530	350	7,171
18	9,256	400	7,157
20	9,036	450	7,146
25	8,640	500	7,137
30	8,376	600	7,124
35	8.188	700	7,114
40	8,047	800	7,107
45	7,937	900	7.102
50	7,849	1,000	7,097

Theoretically, anyone can hold a diversified portfolio. In practice, it is often argued that this is not necessarily possible, because for many private investors not enough capital may be available to carry out such diversification – who can afford to hold hundreds of securities in their portfolio? This argument is not correct. Firstly, even quite modest diversification (say, ten suitably selected securities) can considerably enhance the risk/return trade-off especially if the selection is made using information on the correlation factors. Secondly, given the range of investment funds available via investment management groups worldwide, a very broad diversification is indirectly possible, even for smaller savers. Nevertheless such funds are not a universally popular medium for investment, perhaps because their potential has not always been properly understood.

3. Consequences of diversification

This section will describe in more detail the connection between correlation and diversification. In order to show what the (ex post) risk/return properties of a portfolio look like, we will take a simple example: a US portfolio consisting of IBM shares and GM shares. The data assumed to illustrate this are shown in the following table[1]:

	Return (R_i)	Risk (σ_i)
GM	14.9%	23.4%
IBM	3.5%	19.2%
Correlation of returns (ρ)	0.622	

The table shows that over a specific period, GM shares saw an average return of 14.9% per annum with a standard deviation of 23.4%, while the IBM share averaged 3.5% with a risk of 19.2%.

From the previous section, we already know the definitions of return and risk of a portfolio consisting of two assets:

(i) $R_p = x_1 R_1 + x_2 R_2$

(ii) $\sqrt{\sigma_p} = x_1^2 R_1^2 + x_2^2 R_2^2 + 2x_1 x_2 \rho_{12} \sigma_1 \sigma_2$

where in this example, x_1 represents the proportion of GM shares and x_2 the proportion of IBM shares in the portfolio.

---

[1] Any two shares or other securities can be used here. The qualitative results should be more or less the same.

Now, what are the risk/return properties of the portfolio, if it is assumed that different proportions (x1, x2) of the two stocks are held in different portfolios? The table below gives this information simply by entering the data from the previous table into equations (i) and (ii), assuming different values for x1 and x2.

GM % x_1	IBM % x_2	Portfolio yield R_p	Portfolio risk σ_p
1.0	0.0	14.9%	23.4%
0.8	0.2	12.7%	21.3%
0.6	0.4	10.5%	19.7%
0.4	0.6	8.3%	18.8%
0.2	0.8	6.0%	18.6%
0.1	0.9	4.9%	18.8%
0.0	1.0	3.8%	19.2%

This relationship can also be shown in a chart:

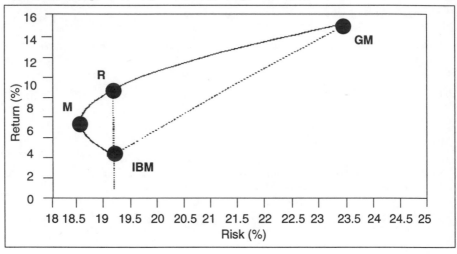

The horizontal axis represents the standard deviation (risk), while the corresponding returns are represented on the vertical axis. The points marked 'GM' and 'IBM' show the combination of risk/return for the two individual shares (ie. portfolios consisting of 100% IBM or 100% GM shares). In contrast, the curve shows the combination of risk/return for mixed portfolios. This curve provides a further confirmation of the results of diversification described above. Contrary to what might be expected on a naive view, the calculated combination of risk/return for a mixed portfolio is not found on the **dotted line** connecting IBM and GM, but on the **concave curve**. This curve shows the reduction in risk which can be obtained via diversification. For example, a 'Minimum Risk Portfolio' (M) could be constructed, taking that combination of all possible GM/IBM Portfolio combinations which shows the smallest risk (the portfolio split here would be around 30% GM and 70% IBM): this would still offer a higher expected return than IBM shares alone. Another mixed portfolio (R) would give a significantly higher expected return but with the same risk as that of the individual IBM share (the split here would be about 50-50).

The above equations show that it is the correlation term which is responsible for this curve. It can also be seen that the dotted line would only be a solution for the combinations of risk/return of a mixed portfolio if the correlation between the returns on the shares were unity, ie. the shares move in perfect sympathy. This is hardly ever found in practice. It follows that in almost all cases, diversification leads to a reduction in the risk of investment, especially, if the chosen shares have very weak, or even negative, correlations.

A two-asset portfolio may be interesting for illustrative purposes, but in practice, of course, more than two securities are typically held – ie. a broader diversification takes place. What are the consequences? To illustrate this, Bank of America (BOA) shares have been introduced in addition to the previous two stocks in our example portfolio. The following chart shows the consequences of this for the possible risk/return combinations.

The chart is similar to the previous one. The horizontal axis shows the risk, ie. the standard deviation of the individual shares, the corresponding returns are on the vertical axis. One curve represents all possible combinations for a two asset portfolio, as discussed above, and the other is the new three asset portfolio. It becomes clear

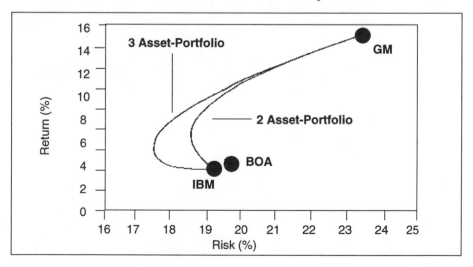

that by introducing the BOA share, once again, the portfolio risk can be significantly reduced. Of course, these graphs are nothing other than an illustration of the fact that by diversification, more and more non-systematic (company-specific) risk can be eliminated. Risk reduction by introducing yet more assets can progress further, until finally only the systematic risk corresponding to the standard deviation of the market index remains.

The following graph is another way of depicting this phenomenon. It shows the behaviour of the portfolio risk, shown here on the vertical axis, against increasing diversification in the Swiss market (example takes bearer shares only). The more different shares are held, the nearer the portfolio risk comes to the pure market risk. It is obviously possible to cancel out most of the non-systematic risk, even with as few as ten shares. The impact of the October 1987 stockmarket crash on market risk is also clearly shown in the graph. The lighter line shows the diversification effect before the crash, the darker line includes the crash period. The 1987 crash was an event which hit all equities almost equally hard, the consequence was an increase in the measured historical average correlation, and thus a decrease in average diversification effects: a phenomenon clearly visible in the chart and a phenomenon which has characterised stockmarkets around the globe. Some investors felt that this almost universal, simultaneous crash in world stockmarkets somehow refuted the logic of global diversification – virtually no investor avoided the phenomenon unless zero-weighted in equities. However, this argument entirely misses the point as it is

Standard deviation

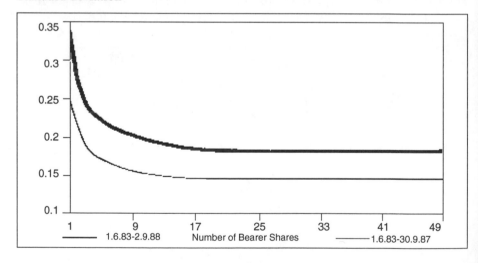

Source: ZIMMERMANN N.H./BILL F.L.M./DUBACHER R.R.: 'Finanzmarkt Schweiz: Strukturen im Wandel', St. Gallen 1989.

not this general risk which can be reduced via diversification but the specific market and stock risks. For example, exposure to the problems and particularly poor performance seen in 1991 in the Japanese and Italian stockmarkets, or in many UK 'cyclicals', would have been limited in a broadly diversified portfolio.

The following table indicates that the possibility of reducing portfolio risk closer to the market or index risk by increasing diversification in individual countries is not only valid in our example of the Swiss stockmarket, but for other markets, too. It shows how many stocks must be held on average in different markets in order to generate a portfolio with a certain overall correlation to the respective index. It is obvious that the rate of risk reduction is not the same in all markets. For example, considerably more individual stocks must be held in the Japanese market than for other markets, in order to achieve the same degree of risk reduction. This is mainly due to the fact that Japanese shares tend to have a greater non-systematic risk than the shares in most other countries.

Number of shares needed to ensure close correlation to market

Portion of risk 'explained' by the market	98%	95%	90%	80%
Australia	121	47	22	10
Germany	99	38	18	8
UK	132	52	24	11
Japan	251	97	46	21
Canada	90	35	17	7
Netherlands	106	41	20	9
Switzerland	98	38	18	8
USA	197	76	36	16

Again, investors may be surprised at how much company-specific risk can be eliminated in a portfolio of just 10-20 shares per market. But we must repeat the message that these cannot just be any 10-20 shares, they should exhibit weak, or negative, correlations. As a 'poor' example, a portfolio consisting of 10 pharmaceutical company shares would typically not fulfil the correlation criterion! A mix of pharmaceutical and construction sector shares may be a better diversification.

4. Efficient portfolios

In theory, it is possible to depict all conceivable assets and combinations of assets in a risk/return chart, as we have already shown for individual assets and their returns. This would, for example, result in a large cluster of points, as illustrated in the following chart:

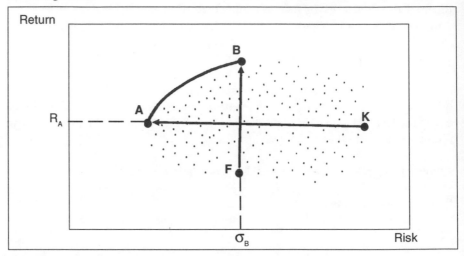

So far, it has always been implicitly assumed that investors prefer:

- a higher yield for the same risk, or
- less risk for any given yield

These two intuitively plausible assumptions in principle reduce the number of possible portfolios which need to be considered, ie. we can reduce the number of viable portfolio combinations. For example, no-one would hold asset or portfolio F in the above chart because there is an alternative investment (B) which would give a considerably higher yield for the same risk. In the same way, no-one would hold investment K, as investment A exists which promises the same yield at a considerably lower risk. Thus, in efficient markets, only investments or investment combinations which lie on the 'envelope' or 'efficiency curve' between A and B would be considered/held. Combinations falling below this line are said to be inefficient.

Furthermore, in dealing with the fundamentals of modern portfolio theory, it has been assumed up to now that only securities with inherent risks exist. However, it has been seen in the section on equity analysis that rather interesting insights can be gained by the introduction of risk-free assets, which actually do exist in reality (eg for all practical purposes, such a risk-free asset might be a short-term Treasury bond or bank savings deposit).

The following chart shows the consequences of the introduction of risk-free assets for the risk/return chart.

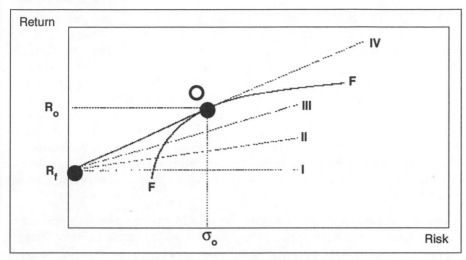

The curve FF is the efficiency curve and R_f is the risk-free interest rate. As the risk-free asset also provides a positive yield, but has a standard deviation of zero, point R_f is the risk/return point for this asset. The straight line starting at R_f and meeting the efficiency curve FF at point O (at a tangent) is called the 'Capital Market Line'. This brings to mind associations with the Capital Asset Pricing Model discussed in the section on equity analysis. The connections will be discussed in more detail in a moment.

What are the viable risk/reward combinations if portfolios may contain both risky and risk-free assets? The lines in the graph starting from R_f and ending at I, II, III and IV show some possibilities. For the same reasons that all points below the efficiency curve in the previous graph were excluded, we can now exclude the lines representing portfolio combinations I, II and III. There is obviously an alternative portfolio for each combination on one of the lines I to III with the same risk but a higher yield. In other words, in efficient markets, the only portfolios to be held even given combinations of risk-attached and risk-free investments, are those shown on the straight line which forms a tangent to the efficiency curve FF. In this way, only the risk-free asset will be held at point R_f. At point O, only the 'market-portfolio' consisting exclusively of investments with risks attached.

It may be helpful to explain again what is represented by the efficiency curve FF. FF represents a cross-section of portfolios – combinations of investments exclusively with risks attached – which promise the highest possible expected return at a given standard deviation (risk). Portfolios containing two or three assets, as shown in the chart in Section 3, will not be typical as most combinations consist of considerably more investments. If we reflect for a moment on the example with IBM shares and GM shares, the efficiency curve would in this case be the line connecting the minimum risk portfolio M and the combination of risk/return on the GM stock.

In addition to this, if we also consider the possibility of holding a risk-free asset, then naturally curve FF no longer depicts the efficient portfolio combinations to the left of O, this simply becomes the straight line between R_f and O. In principle, the latter represents funds which are invested partly in risk-free assets and partly in Portfolio 'O'. It is important to note here that the composition of that part of the portfolio with risks attached does not change even if the ratio of the risk-attached to risk-free assets changes in the total portfolio. In other words, each investor holding assets with risks attached in his portfolio, does so in the form of Portfolio 'O'. How much risk individual investors are prepared to accept no longer determines the composition of the risk-attached securities portfolio. The overall risk is determined only by the proportion of funds held in risk-free assets versus the proportion held in (diversified) Portfolio 'O'.

Optimum portfolio combinations can be calculated given an investor's preference towards risk. After investing a part of the funds in a risk-free asset, and the other part in Portfolio 'O', then the next step would be to determine how Portfolio 'O' is put together. Which investments from the 'investment universe' as defined, and in what proportions, should form Portfolio 'O'? How do we answer this question?

Once more, it would go beyond the framework of this introduction if we were to discuss all the algorithms necessary to determine such a portfolio in detail. For some time, software packages have been available offering a more or less elegant solution to this problem of optimisation. The input needed includes the expected returns on all the different types of investment which should be included in the 'investment universe', and also the corresponding variance/co-variance matrix. The optimisation procedure itself, ie. the calculation of 'optimum' portfolios, in fact presents no great problem, as we indicated already, many user-friendly solution packages are available, but the data and forecasts necessary for the input are much more problematic. Estimation risks will inevitably exist but this does not change the principle of portfolio optimisation. One characteristic of the optimum portfolio 'O' is clear from the diagram: as we can easily see that when the risk free return R_f rises, the risk of the portfolio tends to rise as a higher expected average return is sought. This is intuitively plausible.

Disputes over the determination of optimum portfolios within the framework of modern portfolio theory degenerate rapidly into what should be seen as purely statistical/mathematical arguments, little understood except by experts. This is perhaps the main reason why the corresponding concepts of investment theory have still not become as universally popular, particularly in Continental Europe, as they would seem to merit.

From the start, we have emphasised that we do not want to be excessively formal in following up descriptions of theoretical methods with concrete examples for calculation. In the following table, we have therefore defined an extremely simplified 'investment universe' in order to illustrate the concept of portfolio optimisation mentioned above. We will begin by working with ten US equities. In the table below, we list ten equities with their expected returns over twelve months and their volatility (ie. standard deviation)[1].

	Share	Expected return (R_i)	Volatility (σ_i)
1	Amexco	6%	0.33
2	Boeing	10%	0.28
3	Caterpillar	6%	0.30
4	CBS	5%	0.21
5	Chrysler	8%	0.26
6	Data General	5%	0.23
7	Exxon	7%	0.30
8	Gillette	5%	0.24
9	K-Mart	6%	0.33
10	Safeway	6%	0.21

The corresponding correlation matrix might look like this[1]:

1	1.00									
2	0.26	1.00								
3	0.39	0.52	1.00							
4	0.34	0.58	0.75	1.00						
5	0.47	0.44	0.46	0.42	1.00					
6	0.16	0.36	0.66	0.63	0.33	1.00				
7	0.35	0.42	0.93	0.80	0.31	0.70	1.00			
8	0.59	0.51	0.76	0.61	0.51	0.56	0.71	1.00		
9	0.32	0.45	0.55	0.53	0.22	0.63	0.68	0.75	1.00	
10	0.38	0.52	0.48	0.66	0.29	0.47	0.55	0.44	0.38	1.00
	1	**2**	**3**	**4**	**5**	**6**	**7**	**8**	**9**	**10**

---

[1]   All data used are indicative only and should not be taken as actual estimates over any particular period.

The following graph now shows the risk/reward properties of the individual shares, as well as the 'envelope' or 'efficiency-curve' produced by the corresponding data. As an example, take Point 4, which shows the risk/reward position of CBS shares with an expected return of 5% and a standard deviation of 21%. As risk-free investments (eg a savings account) also exist in our example, we are able to depict the capital market line, and therefore determine a portfolio (M), which defines the composition of the risky part of our total portfolio.

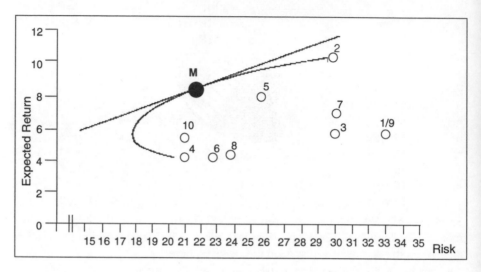

It is clear that the result shown in the above chart is dependent upon the expected returns, and risk assessments, used in the calculations. In this sense, the result for different investors will vary according to their opinions on these key parameters. Portfolio M, the result of our assumptions, has an expected return of 8.5% with a risk (standard deviation) of 22%. It is also worth remembering here exactly what a standard deviation of 22% means in this particular context. It means that we can assume that after 12 months, the return achieved will be in the range 8.5% +/- 22% (always one standard error either side of the expected return) with a probability of 66.7%. That is, there is a probability of 33.3% that after one year the return achieved will lie outside this range. We can also calculate that there is a 95% probability that the expected return will lie in the range (8.5 +/- 2x22%)[1].

---

[1]) See section 5.2 in chapter II on this point.

Within the framework of the 'investment universe' as we have defined it, Portfolio M will look like this:

Portfolio M (R = 8.5, σ = 21.8)

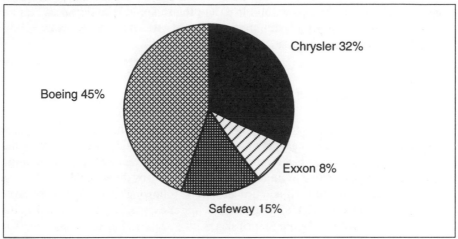

Thus, the portfolio consists of 45% Boeing shares, 32% Chrysler, 8% Exxon, 15% Safeway, and shows an expected return of 8.5% with a risk of 21.8% over twelve months. The composition of this portfolio was calculated using a quadratic optimisation algorithm, the details of which need not be given here[1].

It should have become clear from this example how the theoretic concepts appear in practical applications. In order to carry out such a 'translation', it was necessary to make several simplifications which might appear rather dubious to purists. However, such simplifications are necessary so that non-specialists can gain insight into the concepts, and subsequently apply such methods in their role as investors. It should be stressed that the portfolio structure used in the example would cause problems in practice because the rather narrow diversification still carries a relatively great non-systematic risk. Therefore, the choice of the above 'investment universe', together with the resulting portfolio, should serve for illustrative purposes only.

In a rather intuitive way, our simplified example also reveals the connection between modern portfolio theory and the Capital Asset Pricing Model discussed in the section on equity analysis.

---

[1] The ELTON/GRUBER book, referred to several times already, includes a detailed description of how such an optimisation algorithm works, together with a very detailed bibliography of relevant literature.

In principle, from the theory of efficient markets, the capital market line would be similar to the line in the example given above in the case of the 'investment universe' covering all stocks traded in the market. Under these conditions, Portfolio M (shown above) would be an Index-Portfolio with $\beta = 1$. Portfolios with less risk, $\beta < 1$, would consist in part of risk-free assets, and in part of the Index-Portfolio (thus achieving any specified β). The portfolio with the smallest risk ($\beta = 0$) would naturally consist exclusively of risk-free assets.

5. International diversification

Up until now, diversification has only been discussed in the context of a single country, ie. it has been assumed that only domestic stocks could be held. Correspondingly, the examples given have optimised exclusively domestic equity portfolios. There are, of course, similar arguments for reducing risk by diversification if foreign assets are added to the 'investment universe'. The following chart gives an example of how this might look for a US$ investor. The upper curve shows how the risk in the US market is reduced as the number of shares is increased. If investments are made only in the US, this curve corresponds with the one already shown for Switzerland. The lower curve shows the diversification effects if an investor additionally diversifies internationally, ie. foreign shares are included in the portfolio[1]. It is obvious that by introducing foreign shares into an otherwise domestic equity portfolio, non-systematic risks, here country risks, can again be significantly reduced.

---

[1]   The graph is taken from: BRUNO SOLNIK, International Investments, Addison-Wesley 1988, one of the most comprehensive accounts of international investment theories.

Diversification across a broad range of securities

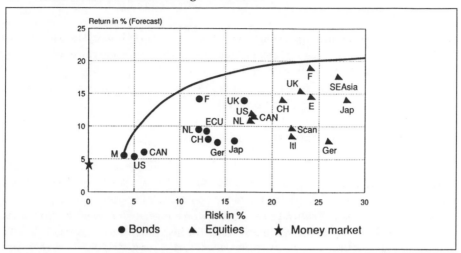

It is clear from the graph that there is a definite difference in risk between equities and bonds. It is not surprising that the US bond market is the investment category with the smallest historic risk, but at the same time the smallest historic return. Furthermore, the efficiency line – drawn above – defines again those portfolios promising the highest yield within each risk class. But now the portfolios are made up of bonds **and** equities, both categories being internationally diversified. In principle, other assets such as property, gold and commodities could be treated in a similar way, however, assessments may be more complicated (eg. there may be non-financial benefits such as 'enjoyment rights').

As we saw in the previous section, it is possible to calculate the exact composition of any portfolio on the efficiency curve.

It is therefore possible, in principle, for any investor to calculate an individual optimal investment strategy, based on individual tolerance of risk. A combination of assets can be selected within which the largest part of the non-systematic risk is eliminated by diversification.

We may have given the impression that in order to follow up such a fully-diversified investment strategy, enormous amounts of capital must be available, because otherwise the degree of 'diversification' would not be possible. In addition, the impression may have been given that passive strategies alone would give peace of mind in investment choice. These arguments will be challenged to some extent in the final section, which deals with the actual realisation of an investment strategy based on the principles described here.

6. The process of investment policy decision making: attempting a synthesis

In this last section, an attempt will be made to use all the basic principles of the theory of financial markets explained in the previous chapters to formulate an investment strategy. This can be thought of as a synthesis of two investment philosophies, the 'Top Down' and 'Bottom Up' concepts. Traditional literature, however, often claims that these two concepts contradict each other.

6.1 'Top Down' versus 'Bottom Up' strategies

The 'Top Down' concept is usually associated with an investment philosophy which starts out examining the economic environment, and via forecasts for interest rates, currencies and financial markets, becomes an investment strategy, selecting markets. In contrast, the 'Bottom Up' concept relies on 'stock picking', usually based on fundamental company or sector analysis, or even chart techniques. The most obvious potential interface between the two approaches is at the sector level, where there are clearly points in common between the largely economic 'Top Down' appraisal and the sectoral performance of industries. However, we should also remember that 'Top Down' portfolio selection should be based on optimisation procedures using estimates of the individual securities' variance/co-variance matrix which requires in turn detailed information on the companies concerned. It may also be necessary for 'Bottom Up' investors to use forecasts for interest and exchange rates in their assessment of individual companies' prospects (eg for multi-nationals, banks or companies with high levels of debt) but, to somewhat exaggerate the position, their selection of investments may be made without reference to any concept of an appropriate market weighting or potential correlations. It is this seeming indifference of the more extreme 'Bottom Up' investors to the weightings and statistical characteristics of the portfolios created by their stock selection that really sets them apart from the 'Top Down' approach. Indeed, an extreme recommendation of the 'Bottom Up' approach may be the single share 'portfolio' although this would typically only be adopted by private investors in conjunction with other, broader, investments (such as separate pension or life insurance schemes) which would thus deliver diversification. Of course, for those fully conversant with all the steps of the decision-making processes, it is possible to see that both 'Top Down' and 'Bottom Up' approaches may well result in similar portfolios although the starting points and priorities appear so different.

Occasionally, these differences in approach are likened to the perceived institutional differences between 'Asset Management Companies' dedicated to rather long-term oriented risk management akin to a 'Top Down' concept and 'Brokerage Houses', which tend to emphasise stock picking. To some extent, the brokers' position is understandable as it is mainly their business to generate turnover in stocks, and it is in their own interest to make as much use as possible of short-term price movements. However, it should be said that not all 'Asset Management Companies' need be dedicated to 'long-term fundamental' or 'Top Down' approaches to asset allocation, although pension and life insurance fund managers tend to be mostly oriented in this direction. Shorter-term or individualistic fund managers can, and do, offer quite different services based on various approaches to asset selection. As far as the individual investor is concerned, personal requirements must be matched with the service offered – necessitating at least a rudimentary understanding of the principles these services are based on.

The methods described in the previous chapters make it clear that formulating a fully coherent investment policy, right down to the individual security which will finally appear in the portfolio, can only be understood as a synthesis of 'Top Down' and 'Bottom Up' concepts. Both concepts play an important part within the framework of investment policy decision-making based on an appreciation of risk management, but they need to be used in a systematic and sensible way.

What might a reasonable investment policy decision-making process look like?

Firstly, we will try to describe the function of 'Top Down' and 'Bottom Up' concepts in a purely schematic way. It can be seen that for both concepts, the methodological principles described in the previous chapters have been incorporated.

To begin with, for the 'Top Down' approach, an analysis of the international economic and political environment is necessary, leading to forecasts for interest rates, exchange rates and stockmarkets, at least for the major economies. By estimating the variance/co-variance matrix of the returns on all investment instruments available and assessing how much individual investors are prepared to accept risk, it becomes possible to develop an international asset allocation, ie. a type of investment-specific optimum portfolio (in equities, bonds, money markets, property, precious metals). At the same time, systematic use is made of diversification, as described in the preceding sections on portfolio theory. In other words, it is possible to determine rather precisely a portfolio which is on the efficiency frontier of a particular investment universe and which is defined by a particular risk profile. We should note that this 'Top Down' procedure is also consistent with the investment philosophy briefly described in the section on Arbitrage Pricing Theory (Chapter III), which could be viewed as a more sophisticated portfolio selection technique than indexation but based on the same diversification principles. More complex analysis of risk factors and exposure (eg. to interest rate or cyclical shocks) can improve efficiency of portfolios and offers the opportunity to bias portfolios in terms of factor risk if judged appropriate. For example, in some periods a bias, or 'tilt', towards interest sensitive shares may be judged appropriate as a means of outperforming a benchmark index.

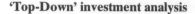

'Top-Down' investment analysis

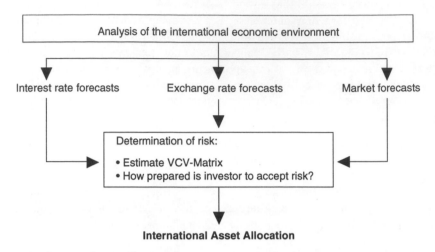

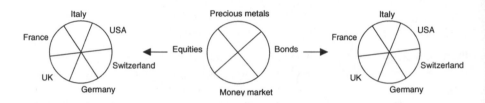

The table gives an example of a combination of forecasts and how they follow on from the analysis of the fundamental assessment of the environment at any given time. The input required consists of forecasts of the most important exchange rates and markets. From these inputs, it is possible to calculate the 'Total Returns' for the various markets and investments from the point of view of the investor (and his base currency). Basically, the risk/return profiles are defined for all investment instruments under consideration, just as they were in the last section, the only difference being that here we are working with estimated expected returns (forecasts), while previously, historical returns were used (these may, however, form the basis of estimated returns). With the help of the estimated variance/co-variance matrix, efficient and optimum portfolios can be calculated. The next two pages show some examples of actual forecast tables (first quarter 1992) for an international investor and corresponding investment strategies for four different risk classes from very conservative (focussing on secure income generation, ie bonds and money market investments only) to aggressive growth (with a greater preference for equities). The tables are from SBC's strategy publication 'The Global'.

Market and currency forecasts: US$ investor

	Market forecast % 12 months	Currency forecast % 12 months	Total return %
Bonds			
USA	6.0	0.0	6.0
Canada	8.3	-1.5	6.6
Switzerland	9.0	-2.0	6.9
UK	15.8	-2.0	13.5
Germany	9.5	-2.0	7.4
Netherlands	11.1	-2.0	8.9
France	14.5	-1.5	12.8
ECU	10.3	-2.0	8.1
Japan	7.7	0.0	7.7
Equities			
USA	11.2	0.0	11.2
Canada	13.3	-1.5	11.5
Switzerland	15.6	-2.0	13.3
UK	18.0	-2.0	15.7
Germany	10.6	-2.0	8.4
Netherlands	14.1	-2.0	11.9
France	21.3	-1.5	19.5
Italy	13.3	-3.4	9.4
Japan	13.7	0.0	13.7

International investment strategy: US$ investor

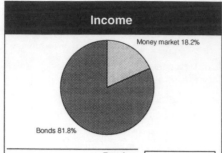

Income

Money market 18.2%

Bonds 81.8%

	Bonds	Portfolio
USA	47.0	expected total
Canada	8.7	return %
Japan	4.3	annualised
Southeast Asia	-	
United Kingdom	3.8	6.8
Germany	3.0	
France	4.3	
Switzerland	2.2	Portfolio
The Netherlands	4.5	long term risk
Scandinavia	-	% annualised
Italy	-	
Spain	-	
Ecu	4.1	
Total	81.8%	4.7

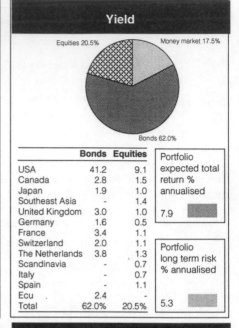

Yield

Equities 20.5%   Money market 17.5%

Bonds 62.0%

	Bonds	Equities	Portfolio
USA	41.2	9.1	expected total
Canada	2.8	1.5	return %
Japan	1.9	1.0	annualised
Southeast Asia	-	1.4	
United Kingdom	3.0	1.0	7.9
Germany	1.6	0.5	
France	3.4	1.1	
Switzerland	2.0	1.1	Portfolio
The Netherlands	3.8	1.3	long term risk
Scandinavia	-	0.7	% annualised
Italy	-	0.7	
Spain	-	1.1	
Ecu	2.4	-	
Total	62.0%	20.5%	5.3

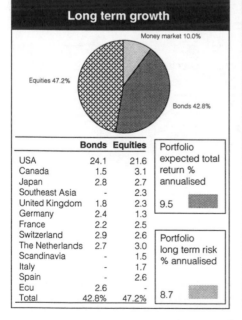

Long term growth

Money market 10.0%

Equities 47.2%

Bonds 42.8%

	Bonds	Equities	Portfolio
USA	24.1	21.6	expected total
Canada	1.5	3.1	return %
Japan	2.8	2.7	annualised
Southeast Asia	-	2.3	
United Kingdom	1.8	2.3	9.5
Germany	2.4	1.3	
France	2.2	2.5	
Switzerland	2.9	2.6	Portfolio
The Netherlands	2.7	3.0	long term risk
Scandinavia	-	1.5	% annualised
Italy	-	1.7	
Spain	-	2.6	
Ecu	2.6	-	
Total	42.8%	47.2%	8.7

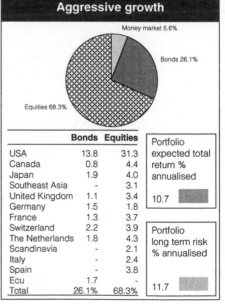

Aggressive growth

Money market 5.6%

Bonds 26.1%

Equities 68.3%

	Bonds	Equities	Portfolio
USA	13.8	31.3	expected total
Canada	0.8	4.4	return %
Japan	1.9	4.0	annualised
Southeast Asia	-	3.1	
United Kingdom	1.1	3.4	10.7
Germany	1.5	1.8	
France	1.3	3.7	
Switzerland	2.2	3.9	Portfolio
The Netherlands	1.8	4.3	long term risk
Scandinavia	-	2.1	% annualised
Italy	-	2.4	
Spain	-	3.8	
Ecu	1.7	-	
Total	26.1%	68.3%	11.7

However, whilst a portfolio may be described as a broad allocation according to type of investment across countries, it must consist of individual securities. Here, the 'Bottom Up' concept comes into play, because we must follow up the question of which individual securities fill the pie charts shown in the asset allocation.

The Index Model and Capital Asset Pricing Model (by estimating risk and stockmarket forecasts) can deliver estimated returns for individual shares. Furthermore, company analysis, coupled with evidence such as that gained from management interviews, gives an indication of whether or not the equilibrium return, calculated from the CAP Model, makes sense. Both concepts are used to formulate a consistent forecast of the expected returns of individual shares in different countries. In addition, by estimating the variance/co-variance matrix of the returns on individual shares, it is possible to attain the country-specific optimum equity portfolio[1]. The following table illustrates this process:

'Bottom-Up' equity analysis

Single Index Model Capital Asset Pricing Model		Management Interviews Company analysis

Risk (Beta) Expected return   Expected return

Optimisation of country specific equity portfolio

Switzerland	Germany	UK	USA
– Nestlé	– Henkel	– BTR	– Dow Chem
– Holderbank	– Karstadt	– Tesco	– Corning
– SBC	– Mannesmann	– Forte	– Merck

Basically the same procedures can be applied for bond markets in choosing individual securities for a complete portfolio, for example by estimating interest rate

---

[1] To optimise country-specific equity-portfolios, it is actually not necessary to estimate the complete VCV-Matrix for all shares. Simpler methods have been developed as described in the technical literature. These lead to approximately the same results as the optimisation using the complete matrix. Key words here are SHARPE-Model or ELTON/GRUBER/PADBERG Algorithm.

profiles. However, some, even quite important, bond markets have extraordinarily poor liquidity (Switzerland falls into this category). This can create problems for achieving theoretical weightings and changes in weightings. Some of the world's small stockmarkets (eg Austria or Taiwan) can present similar liquidity problems, but in the major markets the liquidity problem only arises for smaller companies, and a range of liquid blue chips usually provides a sufficient diversification effect.

The use of both 'Top Down' and 'Bottom Up' concepts here should foster understanding of the fact that these are not substitutes, but should be used to complement each other in a disciplined decision-making process. It should be evident that the application of modern portfolio theory in formulating investment strategy in no way questions the use of sensible financial analysis in assessing companies' prospects. But remembering the theory of efficient markets, the task of financial analysts cannot consist solely of interpreting company reports. It is more a question of identifying and using market inefficiencies in an attempt to outperform the market through selective investments. In the process of pursuing such aims, the analysts will actually 'contribute' over time to the improved efficiency of the market. This can only be done if analysts understand the basics of modern financial theory, because only then can they understand and attempt to identify false evaluations and inefficiencies. If this is not the case, then, from a purely investment oriented perspective, the investor would be better off with a passive strategy, ie with his portfolio weighting corresponding more or less to the market index weighting, than following an analyst's company or market report, however interesting this may be in other ways.

6.2 Active versus passive investment strategies

Apart from the 'Top Down' versus 'Bottom Up' controversy, many see 'active versus passive' as a battleground, representing contradictory views on the practice of investment strategy.

Active strategies are based on the simple assumption that every price in every financial market is not necessarily an 'information-efficient equilibrium price', ie. there are possibilities of achieving outperformance with the help of systematic research. The 'Bottom Up' concept expects such results to come, for example, from detailed company analysis, while the 'Top Down' looks to macroeconomic theories and their application.

In contrast, a purely **passive investment strategy** is based on the view that market prices – be they interest rates, equities, exchange rates or other financial market prices – contain all relevant information. If it is impossible to beat a market index, it is most sensible (and cost-effective!) to use passive investment instruments such as index funds etc.

Fortunately, there is a sensible middle-of-the-road solution just as we found in the combination of 'Top Down' and 'Bottom Up' as described above. On the one hand, the substantial diversification proposed means not being far away from the market index. On the other hand, the recommended strategy is still influenced by forecasts, although the need for diversification guards against excessive reliance on individual forecasts and placing too much faith in these. If only one result from the empirical research in this field were to be accepted, it would be that the forecasting risks in financial markets are very large.

One argument often made against passive investment strategies is the alleged preference of many investors for stock-picking itself, with relatively little thought to risk management or diversification.

This argument without doubt has some truth in it. However, an internationally diversified portfolio does not really exclude investors from holding the individual securities which they have especially taken to their hearts, or about which they have some special knowledge. Diversification really only serves the purpose of not being too far away from the market from the point of view of risk exposure, and controlling non-systematic risks. However, if an investor consciously decides that, in his opinion, some opportunity has a low risk/high reward, then he can exercise his alleged preference, and maybe even 'outperform' the market. By including such an assessment in the estimates of the risk/reward potential of an individual security before buying for his portfolio, he would be justified in his investment choice according to the theoretic portfolio choice. However, this again highlights the estimation error risk we mentioned before.

The only moderate success of passive investment instruments with active managers in Continental Europe is partly explained by the fact that there is felt to be competition between such instruments and the managers themselves. This is due largely to the misunderstanding of the capabilities of both passive instruments and active managers. In professional portfolio management, active and passive components are again not competitors, but complements. It should also be noted that passive investment also requires detailed quantitative research on the part of management companies.

If the theory of efficient markets is right on average, then this does not at all mean that each individual security in the market is 'correctly' valued at every point in time. It is well known that there are many different types of inefficiency in the markets. Here, an active portfolio manager has comparative advantages – he can systematically outperform. The problem with which many active managers have to struggle, however, is that they cannot exclusively concentrate on this specific strategy of 'inefficiency picking', because large portfolios must be broadly diversified and accordingly need constant attention creating time pressures and risks.

Even if the portfolio manager is rather good in his special field, the danger is that under pressure, some neglected parts of the portfolio could perform so badly that the average performance would lie below the index, or the benchmark. A sensible strategy would then be to build the 'core' of the portfolio from index instruments in order to be not too far away from the market regarding risk and return, and to manage a portfolio consisting of specific securities which the manager really understands, around this 'core'[1]. The active portfolio manager should succeed with this strategy in systematically achieving at least the benchmark, which would leave more time to really maximise comparative advantage in specific situations.

There are often objections to strategies such as the above – particularly from an institutional point of view – because they 'de facto' give rise to an index portfolio due to the massive size of some funds and diversification effects. Investigations carried out into institutional equity portfolios show, however, that this is by no means typical.

Mature portfolios, with a more or less regular net inflow of funds, often show structures of risk and correlations which lie far away from the market. This in itself need not be surprising, for example, in Continental Europe, portfolios have typically been managed with hardly any help from quantitative methods. Investigation shows that the size of institutional portfolios does not necessarily lead to indexing. The following chart attempts to answer the question of how far the return on a portfolio with a Beta of one can deviate from an index, taking into account that the correlation between the index return and the portfolio return plays an important part.

Deviation of portfolio return from market return
Assumption: Beta = 1 and Market risk = 20%

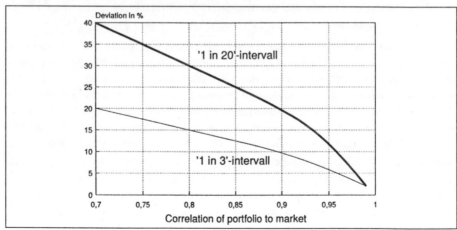

The horizontal axis shows the correlation between the index and portfolio return; the vertical axis represents the expected differences between index and portfolio return.

---

[1] We note that a variation on this solution is a separation of funds managed, so that some managers/ institutions focus on the large, long-term 'core' pool of funds (eg pensions, assurance) whilst others focus on the management of investors' 'non-core' funds and thus tend to be more stock-picking oriented, usually in some defined way (eg 'recovery' or 'small company' or 'green' funds). The end result is anyway the same for investors (provided they understand the difference) even if it creates more polarisation.

The solid line signifies the 'one standard error' range, whilst the dotted line is the 'two standard error' range. We start with a 'Beta = 1 portfolio', a portfolio with a risk corresponding to the market or index risk. The curves show that deviations in performance (positive and negative) result as soon as the correlations between portfolio and index returns deviate from 1. A correlation of 0.8 in one out of three cases leads to a 'performance difference' of more than 15% p.a. (bottom line). However, not only are most institutional portfolios not 'Beta = 1 portfolios', but the correlations, as a rule, are also well below one. The possible (and regular) deviations of the portfolio returns from the index performance will also be correspondingly large.

On the basis of these observations, it therefore seems sensible to construct passive instruments even within an institutional portfolio. Instruments which tie a part of the portfolio to the market in order to generate a close-to-market performance permit the remainder (the portfolio managers' or investors' 'specialities') to attempt to outperform the index. If the 'specialities' are successful, it will be possible, with the help of this strategy, to 'outperform' the market. The fact that institutions have increasingly sought to index a part of their existing portfolios shows that portfolio management is moving in the direction of such quantitative risk management.

6.3 Investment funds versus direct investment

In the introduction it was indicated that the arguments and strategies which we would put forward in this book should be seen as relevant not only for institutional investors, but also, perhaps especially, for private investors. It was also suggested that international diversification strategies have sometimes been viewed as demanding large portfolios. It is again emphasised that such strategies could be implemented quite simply via a range of investment funds. Of course, a private investor will usually not have the means available to directly hold an optimum diversified equity and bond portfolio of individual securities across all different countries. Although it has been shown that, by careful application of the 'low correlation prinicple', a considerable reduction in risk can be achieved in a portfolio even if this only consists of a small number of securities, another solution is to use the country-specific equity and bond funds offered in the markets as vehicles for pursuing an international investment strategy. The investment funds take over from the investor the problem of diversification within markets, thus reducing non-systematic risks. In general such funds are administered by investment specialists well-versed in quantitative and risk management techniques. In this sense, investment funds should be understood to be instruments which enable even a private investor with a relatively small amount of savings to construct a cost-efficient international diversification strategy. Such a fund-strategy would probably give a private investor as well-balanced a portfolio strategy as many an institutional investor, according to financial market theory.

Conclusions